Song of the Sandman
Keep Winning
David Sand

Write Learn and Earn

in
https://sandmandavid.com/

🐦
https://twitter.com/sandmandavid

📷
instagram.com/sandmandavid1/

f
facebook.com/Sandmandavid

♪
tiktok.com/@davidsand82

Dedication

I dedicate this book to all the people in my life, past and present, that have journeyed with me along the path. You know who you all are and even if not named in the book; I am grateful and blessed to have had you in my life.

To my mum Barbara and late father Peter John Sand, thank you for everything.

Above all I dedicate this book to my beautiful wife Dorcas and my amazing two sons Daniel and Nathan. I love you to the moon and back.

Keep Winning

David

A Psalm of David

The Lord is my shepherd; I lack nothing. He makes me lie down in green pastures, He leads me beside quiet waters; he refreshes my soul. He guides me along the right paths for his name's sake.

Even though I walk through the darkest valley, I will fear no evil, for you are with me;your rod and your staff, they comfort me.

You prepare a table before me in the presence of my enemies. You anoint my head with oil; my cup overflows.

Surely your goodness and love will follow me all the days of my life, and I will dwell in the house of the Lord forever.

Acknowledgements

THE PROCESS OF WRITING a book is not an easy one and I want to thank Richard Simmons and his partner for helping me along the way. I also want to thank Kim Vermaak for helping me get this over the line and publishing the manuscript on Amazon. I have much more to write; I'm now at the age of 57 and so much has happened in these last seven years of my life and the intention is to write a second volume that covers more of my business reflections than my personal life but of course the two are so intertwined it would definitely also have in the book personal stories and reflections no doubt.

Foreword

THERE IS NO BETTER way to learn from others than through their stories. Not only do we learn about them and their wisdom, but in the process we also learn more about ourselves. And who better to learn from than a leader and visionary like David Sand.

Reading Song of the Sandman is like a heart-to-heart conversation with David. Although he and I have shared many of those, the book gave me many new insights into his genius and journey. (And a bit more time than his active nature usually allows!)

More than just a memoir, this is an MBA education wrapped neatly into a thrilling page-turner of a story. The lessons are as valuable, and the process is far more enjoyable.

Leadership is a journey, and David's story shows it is ongoing. From his early foundations as an adventurous (and, as we learn, mischievous) Scout to building the global success of Uwin Iwin and captaining the international professional organisation SITE, his lessons from leadership and life hit home. In these pages, he is as generous in sharing the trials and tribulations as he is about the triumphs.

In an era where we are discovering the vital importance of being conscious in everything from consumption to capitalism, from leadership to life, David sets a worthy example. His genuine self-awareness and no-nonsense honesty flow from his core values. Having known him for years, I continue to see those values embodied in his life and work.

David's story also demonstrates how his impact extends from himself and his bedrock faith to his family, company, clients, community, worldwide network and beyond. The respect he has earned in all those circles is testament to a far-reaching contribution. This is a mark of the living, long-term legacy of great leadership.

In your hands, you hold the story of an individual who has wrestled with becoming a conscious leader. Through the peaks and the valleys, he has continued to embody his motto: Keep Winning.

May your life and legacy be enriched and blessed by David's story.

Ian Hatton
Conscious Leadership Expert, International Keynote Speaker and Founder of Totally Morpheus Leadership Development

Contents

Prologue

YOU MIGHT SAY I am in the business of winning... No, I am unable to tell you whether the favourite will win the horse race on Saturday, and I certainly can't give you the Lotto numbers, but winning is my game.

I have travelled many miles, both physically and spiritually, to get to this point in my life and I am glad to say that every day brings new challenges, new inspiration and a certain sense of peace.

Winning is an incredible business. Helping people and companies to achieve new heights will always be my passion. I am fortunate to say that in my business, we help people win and organisations win, and as a result, Uwin Iwin.

But how I got here is my story, and I hope that by sharing some of these trials and triumphs with you I will be able to inspire the winner in you.

Keep Winning!

Introduction

ONE OF THE REASONS I wanted to tell my tale is because it's a story of overcoming and making it against the odds. I want to encourage people that have had either childhood or adult illnesses, or any kind of adversity when it comes to health.

I had a bout of encephalitis as a young child, and I think as a result of that I had several fits and it was diagnosed as Grand Mal epilepsy, and this is something that I had to get medicated for. I didn't really understand it at the time, and I was in and out of hospital as a young kid and didn't get to grips with it until much later in life. Living with epilepsy requires that you regularly go for tests where they plug you into one of these brain scan-type-of MRI machines, they put electrodes all over your head and you look a little bit like a spaceman. It's confusing to say the least. Of course, this had a major impact on my schooling, and I was always a little bit behind as a young child.

I was always slow at reading. In maths I found it difficult to concentrate - probably was ADHD but of course that wasn't in vogue at the time so we just struggled through it - and my mom took me to some of the very best neurologists in town. I was on medication and it certainly helped a great deal. There was a time that they thought that I had grown out of the disease and I stopped all my medication.

Of course, that was fine until the advent of alcohol in my life where I started experimenting, first as a high school kid with alcohol and tobacco and all sorts of other things. The combination of alcohol and lack of sleep was really a huge trigger to bring back Grand Mal epileptic seizures. The first of its type happened during my summer break in my first year at university. We were consuming massive amounts of alcohol, with no sleep, and I crashed my mother's car on the way to a friend's home. I was hospitalised and of course during my time at university I had several incidents. I always looked on the bright side and never saw this as a handicap but rather as something to spur me on, motivate me, show me that I could do it despite this challenge.

I was also always very young in my class, as well as at university, in fact in my first year of university I was 17. For most of my first year it seemed that everybody already had their driving licence and was getting their own cars and getting around. So, I again saw that not as a setback but rather as a challenge, and an opportunity to advance.

Of course, later on in my life when I came to know Christ and found out that there were actually stories of epilepsy in the Bible, where a person is healed from seizures, I got down on my knees and I asked the elders of our church to pray for me. I genuinely believe that God took a huge part of that epilepsy away and provided me with the miracle of not being afflicted with Grand Mal seizures. It's quite a challenge when I see people with epilepsy. When you experience it from the outside, looking at somebody who is having a seizure, it's quite scary. Obviously when you are going through a seizure you are not aware of anything around you and you have a bit of memory loss, so my long-term memory is not as good as it should be. There are bits and pieces of my life I don't remember too much about, but having said that, it is really an opportunity to get through. And also an important motivator for me to write this book.

I remember hearing that Jonty Rhodes was a sufferer, and that he too didn't let that hold him back. He became one of the greatest South African and world cricketers of all time and that was tremendously inspiring. I want anybody who reads this book to know that epilepsy or a similar medical challenge should not hold you back. You can achieve what others have achieved or are able to achieve. Certainly, with today's medical help, with God's help and with understanding how you have to live your lifestyle to help you overcome things, it's really possible to live a full life and to achieve your dreams no matter what your circumstances are.

One

Sand and Savages – My Family

"Family is not an important thing. It's everything." –
Michael J. Fox.

I WAS BORN IN 1966, on the 14th of May, to my father Peter John Sand, and my mother Barbara Ann Sand, nee Savage. They must have been in their early 20s when I was born, and thinking about that it must have been crazy trying to start a career and a life together and then on top of that having a young child. In comparison, my 1st child came when I was 40, almost 20 years later than when they were starting. My dad had started his career as a young sales and marketing chap for a fast-moving consumer goods company, Nestlé, and my mum was a young radiographer. She was a nurse in the radiography unit and a very bright young lady, and I'm sure if she had been given the opportunity she could have qualified to be a doctor had she wanted to go that route, and she often said maybe that's what she should have done.

Dad

My dad had an interesting upbringing. He was the second child of Dorothy and Israel Cecil Sand. Dorothy was a daughter from a Baptist Christian family, and Israel Cecil Sand was the Jewish son of a very devout Jewish family that had its origins back to central Europe; when the Russian Jews emigrated from that part of the world, some of them ended up in South

Africa. Israel was an interesting guy, an entrepreneur, and these two got married at a time it was really taboo to cross the religious, cultural sides and marry, but they did, and that caused a bit of conflict for my dad, in that he desperately wanted to follow his father's religion as the son of a Jewish man. Because the children of a mixed religion marriage like that follow the traditions of the mum, he and his sister Wendy were brought up as Christians. I think my dad really yearned to follow in his dad's footsteps, to be able to go through the rites of passage, Bar-mitzvah and then the various Jewish traditional things that he was unable to do.

When I was born my mum and dad first had a small apartment on Corlett Drive in Johannesburg, and then a year or two later when my brother arrived, we moved to a wonderful little family home in Parkview, in Galway Road. That was a beautiful place to grow up and it still is a wonderful part of Johannesburg.

My dad then joined his father in business. Cecil Sand, my grandfather, was a very bright man. He studied dentistry at Wits University and then didn't want to pursue that, so then he did a commerce degree. He did all sorts of things initially, I think he was one of the founding partners of Premier Milling, or was quite involved there, and then left that to start his own finance company. He called the finance company Peter Pan Investments, after his son Peter, and his daughter Wendy, or Peter and Wendy from the fairy tale Peter Pan. This was a business in which he pioneered factoring and early forms of hire-purchase for small entrepreneurs that couldn't necessarily get finance from the bigger banks because of their credit ratings. This sort of niche financing initiative is obviously, in today's environment, huge, and he as a visionary businessman saw the need to help entrepreneurs finance their assets and potentially manage their cash flow by discounting as still happens to this day.

So, my dad joined his father. My father had quite a privileged education at Hilton, although he hated being a boarder and was bullied. He didn't go to university and I can only assume that he struggled a little bit in his schooling. Nonetheless he was a bright man and he learnt well from his father and he got into the family business, Peter Pan Investments. Unfortunately, as life would have it, his father passed away from a massive heart attack on the bowling green at the Wanderers Club, and my young father was left to run this business, which was quite a complicated one, on his own. I think the death of his father was very traumatic for him and he struggled. Thankfully, my mum's father, his father in law, a very strong dapper Englishman by the name of Harry Savage had reached his retirement age and he came into the business to help my father see it through the difficult times that he had. Harry had been a financial director for Beecham Group, a British pharmaceutical company, and the two of them really did well. I think it was a tremendous input that my father received from Harry. They bonded and managed to grow the business and make it strong. But then they decided that the best thing would be to sell the business to a suitable party. Along came Standard Bank, who had a financing division or hire-purchasing division called Stannic, and Stannic bought the book of Peter Pan Investments. My father secured a mid-management job at Stannic in a corporate capacity. It was very successful in that there was a good sale agreement, and my father was able to put some money aside into a trust for his mother and sister. He was very diligent about investing and looking after that and today my mother enjoys the benefits of that trust and those funds.

My dad however was more suited to the entrepreneurial environment than corporate life, the politics of a corporate structure, and the intensely long working hours and expectations. This meant we didn't really see my father that much after that as he was working long hours, and I remember him grumbling and moaning at the dinner table about people in the workplace being such nasty pieces of work. But along the way my dad always talked about business, he always talked about how things worked and he was very positive, and that had an early childhood impact on myself, aspiring to want to be in business one day. But I do remember, and this connects with my own career, that somewhere along the line, he was put in charge of organising the Stannic incentive programme. The year that he organised it, it was a trip to Spain, and he was the liaison with the travel agent. He had to organise the flights on Iberia which was still flying at the time and he organised a fantastic incentive programme for the Stannic dealer channel and internal sales guys. I remember him coming back from that trip having really, really enjoyed it, so that is probably also something that had a very positive impact on my career. I never knew then, but I would end up in the incentive industry, quite something.

All throughout my schooling, my dad really kept on encouraging me tremendously to do the best I could and try and get into university even though I wasn't a particularly good student. My father loved us so much as children and he always expressed this deep love not only in actions but also in words, and he was really a kind man, as well as being a tremendous encourager. He hated discipline, my mother was the disciplinarian in the family, and we certainly got a fair share of that. My father always said, "we're lovers not fighters in our family", and I've caught myself on numerous occasions telling my sons the same thing.

My dad resigned from Stannic at an appropriate moment, and went to join a friend of his, Brian Houson, in a chemical business as the financial director of that business. That went well for a few years, although I remember him moaning and groaning about trade unions and all sorts of nonsense that they had with workers and their production facilities. When that was all going on, I was going through my university days, I had got into

Rhodes University. He was a tremendous encourager there; he came down to Rhodes a few times and he was really proud that I had made it through and was able to go to university. The other thing that my dad encouraged me to do was to go and get a good corporate job after university. I did that, and I went to work for Anglo American first and then Barlows, a huge blue-chip South African conglomeration of businesses. Of course, when I started my own business again my dad was hugely supportive. Although he was disappointed that I had given up on my corporate career, I do think that he understood why. Right throughout my working life he was always there, and he actually came to work for Uwin Iwin for a while - I'll talk about that again a bit later on - but when my dad passed away it left a tremendous hole in my life. He was a good sportsman - he was a provincial tennis player in his day and a great golfer, and we played many rounds together. He was a guy that I loved deeply, who loved me deeply in return, and was always there to give tremendous support, business advice and friendship.

Mum

My mum was born in Camps Bay. Her father was an expat from England, who married a South African woman, and they had a little home in Camps Bay. Camps Bay was certainly then not the fancy jetset lifestyle that it is today. To the contrary, it was one of the poorer suburbs of Cape Town, and I just wish the family had held onto their real estate asset because today it would be worth an absolute fortune. My mum's parents, my granny and grandpa Harry and Vi Savage, were a tremendous couple. Vi Savage was such a loving woman and she and I had a tremendous bond. I was her first grandchild, she loved me in a very special way and I certainly was her favourite. She lived a long life and I got to spend quite a lot of time with her. Towards the end, it was a very special time when my mum and the family cared for her until she passed.

My mum was schooled at Loreto Convent and she had a great relationship with one of the nuns, Mother Marie Estelle. I remember through our early, mid and late childhood going to visit this old nun who was then transferred up to Pretoria. When my mum came up to Gauteng, or the Reef or the Rand at the time, she kept in touch with this old teacher, and that's really another characteristic of my mother, devout loyalty and commitment.

I always remember my mum as a feisty fighter, somebody that always backed the underdog, worked hard, did her very best for her family, was passionate, protective, and a nurturing mother. Being a Leo, she was also highly protective of her cubs and family and she certainly never backed down from anybody that threatened her or her family. My mum always worked and wanted to contribute to her young family and be supportive of my dad. I mentioned earlier that she was trained as a radiographer, and I think she was very efficient at that, she loved doing her work. She could have probably expanded her medical career if she had taken on the opportunity to study and grow.

I think my mum stopped her career in radiography when she started to have children. After she had had my brother, and my sister Marion, she took up a half-day job at the Wanderers Club which was tremendous for us as little kids as we got to enjoy the club facilities when it was still a vibrant social environment. My mum and dad played tennis, and we enjoyed the beautiful big swimming pool and all the fields. Of course, in those days we could be let loose in the safe environment of the club, and ride our bikes and really have a great deal of fun at the Wanderers Club.

My mum was the disciplinarian in the house and didn't hold back on a good belting. She had her favourite – we had an Alsatian that we had adopted along the way and he came with this beautiful leather strap lead that she would often threaten to belt us with. Then if we hadn't corrected our behaviour she would actually go and get that belt out of the kitchen cupboard, and chase after us with intent, and we did get it a few times, that's for sure.

My mum was always a tremendous cook and great entertainer. She loved entertaining people in her home, she loved cooking, and she taught all three of her children to cook and I think we really appreciate that. My brother went on to make a career in cooking. He's a highly qualified chef and runs a catering and conference business.

So we really enjoyed growing up – my mum was a very practical woman, she loved getting us involved in all sorts of activities or sports and we also joined the boy-scout movement. My brother and I joined the cubs, and later moved on to scouts. There is a tremendous amount of parent involvement there and she helped us get through our cubs and Leaping Woolf. Then later through my scouting career I achieved the highest honour of Springbok Scout. That was a tremendous journey along my life that I am very grateful to my mum for, for having introduced us to all that and having supported my brother and I through our scouting life.

Mum also struggled in my early childhood with my health issues. It must have been very tough for a young parent to see a child suffer with that kind of a condition, although she was always very patient with me and helped me find the very best medical care in South Africa, and virtually through some very difficult times. Again, just such gratitude for my mother and what she did and how she did it. I must say that it is a huge sacrifice from her, that growing up as a child you don't always appreciate but you do appreciate immensely when you have children of your own.

I am very lucky to still have my mum alive and well. She's a very active bowler, she can get around a golf course but that's not really her thing, and she's a tremendously good bridge player. She taught us all how to play bridge very early on as a card game, along with all sorts of other card games and fun board games and things like that. As you can tell, our relationship was and still is a very special one.

Nigel

My earliest memory of my brother Nigel is the two of us playing in the garden of our home in Parkview. We had this little Indian tee-pee that we had got for Christmas or a birthday, and we spent hours in this little tepee playing cowboys and Indians and running around. He was a tremendous little chap and the two of us really had a fantastic start to life. Our cousin Kevin and his sister Bev lived next door, and Kevin was more my brother's age, or kind of in the middle of the two of us, so he was friends with both of us. We used to hop over the wall and play and build forts together and do all sorts of things that we shouldn't have been doing.

I remember in those days every parent and aunty and uncle smoked like crazy. Smoking was not deemed to be unhealthy and at every big party, people were smoking. One little story I remember of my brother and Kevin at one such party is this: the adults had gone through from where they were sitting in the lounge area to the dining room, and the kids had eaten earlier. The adults didn't take their cigarettes to the dining room table, so all these packs of cigarettes were everywhere and the two of them went around the room basically taking one cigarette out of each box. I think they collected ten to fifteen cigarettes that way, created a stash and got a box of matches, and they decided that we were going to go and start smoking. We coughed our lungs out that day but thought it was pretty cool. My brother and

Kevin decided that they needed a little smoke break a few days later, and they got up onto the small guest loo and opened the window that was high above. Hanging in front of this little window was a net curtain and they thought it would be a great idea to burn holes in the net curtain as they were having their little smoke break. Nonetheless my mum caught them, and really lashed into them for their bad behaviour, for their smoking and most of all because she was terribly upset about her net curtain! But that was Kevin and Nigel and we all had lot of fun. We rode bikes everywhere; we fell off bikes, had our first stitches from our bikes, and had a really good time together.

Growing up, always being a couple of years ahead, I was quickly distanced from my brother and sister through education structures – when I was at junior school, he was at crèche, when I was in high school, he was in primary school, when I was at university, he was at high school and so in a way I always felt quite separated from him through the schooling system. When I went to university, my brother was growing up, he was finishing off his high school and he got involved with a very different set of mates and he started going his own direction. Nigel then went the hotel school route, became a fantastic culinary chef and started his path in life. Nigel is a tremendously talented sportsman, I think he gets that from my dad. He was a provincial squash player and now plays veteran squash and is very active, has a single figure handicap at golf, and I must say I am very jealous about that because I am just nowhere near as competitive as he is on the sporting field. But we have a great relationship now and both being in an entrepreneurial space can support each other where my dad used to support both of us separately.

Marion

Being separated by about 5 years in age, my sister Marion and I were of course even more distant, with her being the little girl in the family. I remember being really fascinated with this little girl, and she of course caused her own challenges for me because she was always rather prim and proper, a compliant child whereas I was not, anything but! This little "rugrat" used to tell mommy exactly what we had done and not done on a regular basis, and I think I got into a fair bit of trouble because of Marion. She's a very kind-hearted, gentle individual and it's very, very hard not to love somebody like that. She always was that way inclined, and I think of my relationship with Marion now, it's one in which we really care for each other greatly, we also share deeply in our commitment to our Lord and saviour, Jesus Christ. I remember becoming born again and praying for Marion and her family, and it was with great joy that I learned a couple of years after that, that her family had given their lives to Jesus in a meaningful and significant way. Her husband Glen, and her two boys, Gareth and Murray Waldeck, are deeply involved in a church in Pretoria and we share our faith and pray for the rest of the family, and certainly grow together in being able to share our experiences and what God has done and blessed us with.

Marion went to St Mary's school in Johannesburg, and that was always something that I used to tease my dad about – my brother Nigel and my sister Marion were afforded a private school education where I had to slum it out at King Edwards High School, which of course was a phenomenal school and still is today. I always used to tell my dad "Ja, you spent all this money on my brother and sister, and they didn't even go to university!" I was the only one that went to university, so I used to tease him that he had wasted his money on my siblings, sending them to private school. These comments infuriated him and I'm sure it hit a nerve.

My sister married a metallurgist, Glen, and they met in Simon's Town on a family vacation – my mum and dad used to rent a beautiful little house in Boulders Beach, just the other side of Simon's Town. We used to have our family holidays down there, my dad would put the car and all of us on the train which we didn't like that much because it took so long. We'd get off the train in Cape Town central station, drive the car off and carry on down to Simon's Town. In hindsight it was actually such a cool way of doing a family holiday! We got to play cards, chill out and meet some other intresting people on the journey.

Anyway, that's where Marion met Glen. He was a young cadet at the Naval academy or at the Naval base down there, serving his two-year military service, and she met Glen during one of the holidays, Marion must have been just out of high school then. They got married and had two fantastic young boys.

Grandfather Harry Savage

On reflection, my grandfather Harry Savage had quite a big impact on me as a young boy. He was a strong man; he was a man of not many words but he certainly had a tremendous presence and character. He was clearly a leader, although I didn't know it at the time. He led both in the organisational context, as financial director of a big multi-national, and also in his social and sporting career or environments he was a leader. Harry became chairman of the Wanderers Bowls men's section at a time when there were several hundred bowlers at the Wanderers Club. He was a man of great organisational skill, and he certainly helped my dad with the business when my father's dad passed away.

But the other thing that really caught my eye about this mountain of a man, Harry Savage, was that he was completely bald and I'm probably going that way quite soon. He also always drove the very best Mercedes Benz that he could get his hands on and I remember early on in life admiring this steel-grey, beautiful Mercedes Benz. I'm not sure exactly what it was, but I remember it having red leather seats and a beautiful ivory coloured steering wheel, whitewall tyres and these beautiful fins at the back of the car. I do think I might have got my own passion for Mercedes Benzes from him.

Besides that, he was also an interesting fellow - he collected art, stamps, and coins. His apartment in Birdhaven, which bordered the Wanderers Club where he so loved to spend many of his retirement hours playing bowls, was a veritable collection of South Africa's great painters including a Tretchikoff and several Roweth's, and other artists he had collected on his travels. I have one or two of his collection now and he also had this most incredible wrist watch, it was a gold Bucherer Swiss watch that inspired my love for watches – my grandmother gave it to me and I'm very proud to have that in my watch collection.

Harry was a very international man, he was a man with great character and qualities, he enjoyed a fine cigar; he had a wonderful collection of wines and cognacs and a beautiful art deco booze cabinet that he really loved. My aunt Brenda has that cabinet now.

Just thinking about it, it's quite interesting; my grandfather Harry did have a big influence on my life as a paternal role model.

Two

Growing Up – Primary school

"It takes courage to grow up and become who you really are." - E.E. Cummings

BY THE TIME I had reached the age of primary school attendance, my mum and dad had moved from their small Parkview home to a slightly larger home in the suburb of Bramley. Bramley today is quite close to Alexandra Township – and it was a very middle-class environment and a wonderful place to grow up. We had a big garden with a tremendous rockery because part of the property was on a bit of a hill or slope. When my mum moved the family in, she got stuck into this garden that was covered in brambles and a blueberry sort of thorn creeper all over these rocks. She and our trusted gardener Phineas Dekhutla set about getting rid of this bramble. I remember as more and more of this foliage came out, so these beautiful boulders and incredible places to hide and play and build little caves and dens and all sorts of things emerged, and it was really a fabulous environment to grow up in. The back of the property was bordered on St Catherine's Anglican Church, and a small graveyard. That was also a source of many good stories and fun scaring the living daylights out of friends that were a bit spooked out by the graveyard, and my brother and I used to pull some rather nasty tricks on unsuspecting friends for the first time. But anyway, when we moved into the suburb, the local primary school was Bramley Primary and I started there in Grade One. It was an interesting little school, with a very healthy mix of Jewish and non-Jewish students, probably a good 50/50 mix in those days. Of course, all the pupils were white, because it was in the apartheid schooling structure. Today I am sure it is almost a hundred percent black students that would frequent that school, and I am so chuffed that that's the way it is now.

I was never a fan of the schooling system. I suppose this was because I always struggled a little with my studies, and with my schooling, but I remember at Bramley Primary there was a great emphasis on sport – it was very competitive, especially amongst the Jewish kids. In soccer it was very difficult to get into a good team, but I played soccer and swam for the swimming team and it was a great fun little school. I remember all the fads of yo-yos and marbles and ironies and all sorts of things that occupied us. There was also a lovely little corner café not too far from the school, that we could ride our bicycles or walk to, and we spent many, many, good days there. Later on shopping centres on Louis Botha Ave grew in popularity; there was a shopping centre called Corlett City, and Corlett City had a little ice-rink in it. Towards the end of primary school especially, we used to go up and ice-skate often and we spent many young days hanging out, making friends and making trouble and enjoying the ice-skating, it was tremendous.

$$\bullet \; \bullet \; \bullet \; \bullet \; \bullet \; \bullet \; \bullet \; \bullet \; \bullet \; \bullet$$

One of my very interesting early childhood memories was that we teamed up with a gang of guys in the neighbourhood, Jonathan Hardham, Andrew Kendal and names that I can't remember any more, but we really had a cool gang of bicycle riding guys. We had a veld nearby that we used to go to and build little forts and whatnot in; and there were the other bunch of guys that were the Jewish clan. We weren't necessarily the best of friends, there was a bit of rivalry and territorial action going on, in the veld especially. One day we had what we'll call a little gang match-up and it was so much fun – one of our guys got his horse and he rode into battle with this horse, chasing the guys out of the park. One of the Jewish guys had a small motorbike and we were throwing sticks and stones and mud pies and all sorts of things at each other – it was a tremendous show-down!

· · · ● ● · ● ● · · ·

Growing up in Bramley was a wonderful experience and like many South African homes, we had the privilege of having a domestic worker. She cleaned the house, sometimes cooked, was always there to help us get ready for school, bath us when necessary and obviously take care of us when mum wasn't at home or was out shopping – she was our babysitter and Nanny.

The particular lady who looked after us was Anna, and I don't remember her surname, but Anna was a gentle, wonderful, nurturing Nanny. She lived on the property in very comfortable quarters. She loved making very, very sweet tea, and she used to make this tea in an aluminium jug with plenty of milk and many spoons of sugar. When she made tea for herself, she usually cut two or three very thick slices of white bread and would dunk the white bread in the tea, eat it and drink the tea at the same time. It was something that I remember so clearly, and we loved eating and drinking it just like Anna did. She was such a caring, kind-hearted woman, and she had a son, his name was Elias. We met him on very rare occasions when he was able to travel from his schooling environment and come and stay with his mum. Anna was a wonderful woman and she helped make our childhood a very pleasant one.

· · · ● ● · ● ● · · ·

We also had some tremendous house pets. We had a beautiful Alsatian -Hero, then at one time a huge long-haired St Bernard - who was also a beautiful dog, and then a Labrador. I remember the Labrador's name was Digby, because one of my friend's father's names was also Digby. The first time that this guy's father came to pick him up of course this little black Labrador went running off to the front door, barking and going crazy as he always did, and we were shouting on the other side "Digby! Digby, stop it! Stop it, stop it, Digby, Digby, Digby" and of course Richard's father Digby was on the other side of the door and he didn't exactly know whether this was a positive greeting or not. We had a big laugh after that when he then told us his name was also Digby. We laughed and laughed also because we thought it was a rather strange name for a man, because we could well understand it was a good name for a dog.

I've always grown up with dogs, and we have always had beautiful Great Danes in our home. I couldn't imagine life without furry companions in the household.

Three

Cubs and Scouts

"A week of camp life is worth six months of theoretical teaching in the meeting room." - Robert Baden-Powell

IN THE NEIGHBOURHOOD AROUND Bramley, there was the 1st Bramley Scout and Cub group that also played a huge part in my upbringing. I enrolled in Cubs at an early age; this was during primary school years. Then as I got into high school I moved up into the Boy Scouts, actually not even in high school - I think it was at the age of about 11 that I moved up into the scout troop. I finished my scouting at about 15 or 16, when I completed my Springbok Scout badge, the highest badge in the scouting world in South Africa.

Scouts and cubs played a huge part in my life. It helped me really grow as a young boy and started teaching me leadership lessons very early on. The whole aim of scouting is to equip young boys, and now young boys and girls, with life skills, so that they can reach their full potential. It's also an outdoor pursuit, and in our beautiful land of South Africa, there were many camps, with amazing opportunities to go hiking and walking, understand wildlife, birding, being able to be equipped with survival skills, first aid training and so on. Of course my love for cooking started in the scouting movement where we learned to cook, both at home and outdoors. It really was a wonderful way of being entertained and learning at the same time. For me that was certainly the best way of learning, it's a style of actively participating in the learning emersion, of being able to feel it, smell it, taste it, experience it and then learn from your successes and your failures, in a safe environment with the mentors and coaches that are around you.

Don't be fooled, scouting wasn't all angelic. I learned how to smoke at scouts; I drank alcohol for the first time at scouts, really misbehaved and got up to a lot of mischief. But I suppose at the end of the day it was an environment that was great fun and I am so pleased I was part of it. What really impressed me was the leadership aspect of the Scouting movement - even as a cub, you get promoted to being a seconder and then a sixer, which is the leader of a group of 5 or 6 guys. The same happens in the scouting environment, you progress and the goal is ultimately to become a patrol leader and then maybe even the group scout. Looking back on that, there were some amazing times. One of the highlights for me was night hiking where we ran the route to various checkpoints. It was extremely physically demanding, and technical in terms of map reading and compass directions, but very exciting at night.

The other stand-out highlight was when our District Commissioner pulled all the scout troops together to do a huge record breaking pioneering project near Edenvale. This was the construction of a drawbridge or a suspension bridge made out of poles, timber, ropes and lashings. I think it was a world record, although I am not 100% sure of that. We spent every night of a long weekend lashing hundreds of poles together, alongside all the other troops, and it was mind-blowing when one of the adult scouters was able to drive his 4x4 vehicle over this bridge. I think it had a span of almost 120m with towers that were 60-odd metres high on both sides of the suspension. It was an incredible project and I only wish I had the photographs of that. It was certainly an amazing standout project of epic proportions and I was glad to be part of that.

Four

KES – My High School Days

"The roots of education are bitter, but the fruit is sweet."
– Aristotle

KING EDWARD THE SEVENTH (VII) High school, in Upper Houghton, was where my Grandad Cecil Sand went to school, and I got in because he was an old boy. Relatively speaking, it was quite close and en route from Bramley into the city where my dad worked in Braamfontein. He would drop us off in the mornings and then we'd either ride our bicycles back, if we had loaded these into the boot, or we'd catch the bus back down Louis Botha, all the way down to Bramley and then walk home from the bus stop. At the time my mum worked at the Wanderers Club, until about lunchtime, so she would also be able to come and fetch us if we were hung up at school playing sport in the afternoons.

King Edwards was a challenging school for me. It was very in favour of sporting accomplishments, so if you did well at sport and made the First teams then you had a good life. It also had a fairly good academic stream, but if you fell anywhere in the middle, not academic and not sporting, then you were relegated to the lower leagues at school, and unfortunately that's where I was. I think from Standard Six or Form One as we called it, to Matric, Form Five, I was either in One 'E' or 'F', one level up from the woodwork class...and of course a fine collection of misfits found themselves in the 'E' and 'F' classes.

At King Edwards the majority of the school pupils were day scholars but there were also two boarding houses on the property which are still there today, School and Buxton House. There was a good collection of boarders as well, some who went home on the weekends and others that were out-of-towners who only got home at the end of term. It was a really traditional school, you greeted the teachers "Sir" and "Ma'am" and if there were any parents nearby you would also make sure that you took your cap off. The uniform was blazer and tie, and it was a school that taught polite manners, proper customs and good values. There were even Latin classes and everybody studied, and again in those days, it was only white boys at the school, under the apartheid government. KES was not a private school, but rather a government or model C school. It attracted a wide variety of kids from both very privileged backgrounds, from suburbs such as Houghton, and Rosebank, to some very poor families that lived in Hillbrow, Yeoville and the Rocky Street areas, and plenty of other children in between.

There was also a wide cultural mix of children, Jewish, Portuguese, Italian, Greek, but mostly white Anglo-Saxon types that I suppose our family fell into. A big school memory was that I was always a small guy, and although I myself was never bullied, I had heard all these stories of my father having been bullied at boarding school at Hilton. I was certainly determined not to have the same done to me, so I got some of the biggest and most thuggish mates that I could and made sure that I was always surrounded by good quality individuals that could support me if the chips were down. Andre being the biggest, he was from a German family and his nickname - Oblex

For me school was not a wonderful experience, they weren't the best days of my life, as many people say they are – I rather look back on my varsity days as the days I really relish as the best days of my education. I always got into trouble, I got jacked numerous times, for all sorts of misdemeanours, and I met some interesting guys along the way. I remember early on a young friend of mine died from a drug overdose, and that really scared the living daylights out of me with regards to drugs and drug abuse. I must say that I've always stayed away from any hard drugs or drugs that could lead to deep addictions, and I'm grateful for that. I suppose that experience taught me something at least, but I was nearly expelled with a number of boarders who grew marijuana at the hostel and were caught smoking it. I think 12 guys got expelled that day, and of the 14 that were on suspicion, I was one of only two that were not expelled and I was again very grateful for that.

KES was for me quite a trying environment. In those days Jo'burg was quite tough socially. Going out and partying very often ended up with one bunch of guys brawling with another bunch of guys for some reason, but that was what it was. I think many of us that are still connected now from our schooling days have a similar reflection on that time of our lives.

Although I didn't play good cricket or rugby, I did enjoy playing in some of the lower level teams. Unfortunately I got kicked in the head very badly during a rugby match against one of the Afrikaans schools and sustained quite a bad concussion. Epilepsy and concussion aren't a good combination and I was not allowed to play rugby after that. So instead I got involved in other extra mural activities, and golf was one of the things that I did find a bit of a niche with. My father was a very keen golfer, so he taught me to play golf and there was a little golfing fraternity at school. We used to play down at Houghton, or Killarney, as and when we could get opportunities as a school golfing team to go and play. That really set me up for a lifelong pursuit of the sport of chasing a little white ball in beautiful environments.

The other extra mural activity that I really got into, when it first grew in popularity, was the sport of windsurfing. In our school we had a guy who went on to become a South African champion and I think he even went to the Olympic Games when windsurfing became an Olympic sport. His name was Torn Masterson and he was a great guy. Torn introduced some of us to the sport and we used to go windsurfing at all sorts of funny places. Jo'burg's not a great place for wind, but later on in my varsity days I got down to the coast and bought some coastal windsurfers. There I was able to extend my love of windsurfing to the coast and wave riding and that kind of thing, with a group of varsity buddies.

The other reflection I have of my school life is how a teacher had a huge impact on me. My Standard 9 and matric teacher was a guy by the name of Mike Edie and he was our history teacher. He truly was an exceptional teacher. He knew that he was teaching not the top 'A' students, but the bottom of the barrel, and he managed to inspire us as a class. '5E' was our matric class and I had this horrible nickname of "Veg" or "Vegetable" because I would just zone out because of my medication and my epilepsy. I didn't always get things and was a bit slow so some of my wonderful friends gave me the nickname of "Veg". Anyway, Mr Edie as he was known to us, was really a superb teacher and he was the only teacher that we, or I came across certainly, that was able to inspire us to want to do better than we were doing. He actually went on to become headmaster of St John's and other great private schools. I know he's a top educator today, and I certainly want to say a thank you to Mike for getting me through Matric with enough marks to qualify to get into university. I bumped into him on the squash court at Rhodes university playing squash one day. He was going into the court and I recognised him and he recognised me and he said "What are you doing here?" and I said "Well I'm attending Rhodes University" and he said "My goodness, I'm so pleased to hear that!" Nobody in the school expected anyone in "5E" to go to university but there were a handful of us that did. I was very proud of that.

I mentioned that I had made friends with some tough guys at school. Andre was a big German guy, who had a tough father and interesting household upbringing. Andre was nicknamed Obelix after the character in the Asterix cartoon series, and he was a huge guy that could really move mountains and intimidate anybody. There was another mate Mark Bennett who lost his eye doing something crazy with melting lead from the necks of wine bottles. His experiment exploded in his face and he lost his eye. There was also Ryk Cloete, he was a borderline kind of guy – he was a bit of a jock but he also fitted in with our crowd quite well, and he was a really cool guy. Grant Sandham, whom I still know to this day, works in the hotel side of the hospitality industry now as a top event guy. Another interesting friend was Steven Burrell whose dad was a top attorney, specialising in patent law. They had a huge house in Houghton, and Steven had a very privileged upbringing. Steven and I were good mates and we enjoyed some of the privileges that his dad was able to shower on us as kids growing up. Another that I remember was Steven Kraut the boxer, who was a tough Jewish guy, he loved boxing and was sometimes misunderstood.

After our 35-year reunion it's been great getting to know all the guys again and thanks to Facebook we can now stay in touch wherever we are in the world.

Five

Smokers' Corner and Love of Rugby

"It's not whether you get knocked down, it's whether you get up." – Vince Lombardi

AT SCHOOL I HAD started smoking and my dad couldn't understand how I was the first up and into the car, with my bicycle packed. I would then shout at my brother to get a move on so we could get to school but the real reason I wanted to get to school early was to have my first Chesterfield of the morning! We rushed into school and ripped down to "Smokers' Corner" which was a little ablution block next to the arts class. We'd have a smoke and then steam into assembly before the bell stopped ringing, reeking of smoke. We would walk past teachers and of course they knew that we had been smoking but we thought we were invisible to them. Smoking at school wasn't cool but that's what happened and it was part of my school days.

I obviously couldn't be a rugby player, but I certainly loved watching the First Team play. It was mandatory during the season to always attend the First Team rugby matches. King Edwards High School had a war cry that was absolutely spine chilling and hair-raising – I think it even rivals that of the New Zealand Haka! When the First Team runs onto the field and that war cry is proclaimed, and sung and shouted out from the benches, what an emotionally stirring start for any team getting onto the rugby field and it must have been quite intimidating for the rival teams. Today I am an avid rugby fan. I support the Lions in South Africa, and I love watching

World Cup rugby, and certainly the big international matches. I support the Springboks with all my heart – my blood is green, and I'm sure that my love for rugby and love for the game in general stems back to my school days.

· · · ●·●· ● · · ·

Another memory from my school days – I was introduced to the music of Bob Marley and I became a bit of a wannabe Rastafarian. I used to wear the Rasta colours on my blazer, three red, yellow and green pins stuck into the top of my lapel. We used to really love Bob Marley, and there were a couple of us that shared this Rastafarian passion in the smokers' corner gang. We did experiment a little with weed, in high school and through my varsity days, but that was only at the end of Matric. So crazy that now that's been legalised.

My Matric dance was an absolute disaster but then my dating girls seemed to be a disaster in general. I think my 1st date with a girl was with the rugby coach's daughter and that was not ever going to be successful. On this date I took her to the movies. After that we sat down and had a little hamburger and a pink milkshake each and I, through my nervous hand gesticulations, knocked the pink milkshake into my food, and my chips and my hamburger were floating around in that mess. I really didn't recover well from that and so I didn't pursue very many girls at high school, but certainly enjoyed the good parties and dancing and socialising. I suppose I grew up a little bit faster when I hit Varsity. I managed to scrape a good enough Matric pass to get enough points to get into Rhodes University, then the next leg of my education journey continued.

Six

First Love

"First love is a little foolish and a lot of curiosity." - George Bernard Shaw

I MET A GIRL called Libby during my matric year and she became my girlfriend. We had a great year together during my matric year and we went to her school dance. It was not her Matric Dance because she was a standard below me – but it was fantastic. We went in her father's Alfa Romeo, he lent us his vehicle and we had a cool time. I don't think I need to say too much more about that, but I must say she and her family were very good to me and we carried on dating on and off throughout my university time. Many people may have thought that we would have ended up getting married, but it wasn't to be. We had quite a big break up after university, or in my final year, I'm not sure exactly when it was. We were down in Ballito on the Natal North Coast, and I embarrassed myself quite badly, and so ended my relationship with my first serious girlfriend.

Seven

Rhodes – Jo'burg Boy Hits Small Town Blues

"A ship in a harbour is safe, but that is not what ships are built for." – John A. Shedd

I SPENT MY FINAL school holiday in Simon's Town, in a beautiful place called Boulders Beach, where my parents rented a home for the holidays. There I anxiously awaited the publication of the Matric results. I desperately wanted to go to university and get a good qualification, and my dad had that dream for me as well . He had always encouraged me to try and get into university. When the big day finally arrived, I was greatly relieved to hear that I had passed, and I had gained enough points for a university exemption. So there was a huge celebration that year. I think we partied almost every night thereafter and it was probably one of the biggest New Year's Eve parties that I've ever had, shared with my family and friends. It was a great time - I felt on top of the world and nothing could stop me. Then it was back to Jo'burg to catch up with my old school mates that had also passed, some had done well, some hadn't done so well, and we were now going to make our way into the big wide world. We were all sitting around, drinking and socialising, when my dad phoned and said "Son, I've got great news. You've been accepted into Rhodes University, and we have to go and get ready, because in a few days' time you're going off to an induction week at the university before it starts." What a fantastic moment, for both myself and my dad who had believed in me all along.

So I had said goodbye to all my mates and within a couple of days we were in the car on our way down to Grahamstown. I had no clue where Grahamstown was, and I had even less of a clue about what Rhodes University was about, other than I knew it was a good place to go and it was one of the first universities that had accepted my application. I think I had applied to Rhodes University, Pietermaritzburg University, and Cape Town; Rhodes was the first to come back and say they had a place for me, so my next stage in life was set.

My parents and I drove down south with a fully packed car. It took 12 long, long hours, and finally we saw a sign that declared there were 25 kms between us and Grahamstown. That's when I thought "My goodness, this is absolutely in the middle of nowhere! How am I going to cope? I'm this big Jo'burg city boy, going to the middle of nowhere that takes 12 hours by car to get there..." Anyway, we drove into Grahamstown, but we came in via the township which was on the main road, and I thought "Oh wow, this is where I am going to spend the next 3 years of my life." It was a horrible entrance from that direction through the old township. There is of course now a bypass road that goes round it, but driving in I wondered what I had got myself into. We drove up through the town. There was a huge big cathedral, a very short main street and then the entrance to the university. So my first impression of Rhodes University and Grahamstown was just not a good one, and I said to my mom and dad, "I really don't think I'm going to be able to cope staying here for 3 years!"

Anyway, after 4 years I had thoroughly enjoyed the place and was ready to go back to Jo'burg, but there are many other stories before we get to that point.

• • • • • • • • •

Winchester House

1984 was the year that I arrived in Grahamstown and having completed a pre-university induction course for two weeks, I moved into my residence which was Winchester House, part of the Salisbury Hall. Winchester House was a small residence of forty-four students, and really a cool little place to get to know plenty of guys in a meaningful way. On arrival I still had a bit of the big city attitude that was born out of needing to survive at school and of course I took that sort of Jo'burg attitude down to the Eastern Cape which was totally inappropriate. After a couple of days of observation, one of the senior guys, a man that is still a dear friend today, Grant Sellick, pulled me aside and said "Dave, you know you don't need to bring this Jo'burg aggression down here to Grahamstown, you just won't make any friends that way." He was a Jo'burg boy himself, having been to Parktown Boys High School, and we chatted and swapped stories and what he had said really sunk in and I went on to meet some tremendous mates at Winchester House.

Rhodes Political Tension

Rhodes was a melting pot of so many different cultures and races, and of course it was right in the pre-democracy era, where the tensions were running very, very high. The Eastern Cape was a hotbed of political activity. Fort Hare, our sister university, was close by. It was one of the only black universities that was producing graduates and it was a source of political unease. At Fort Hare and at Rhodes there were lecturers and leaders and liberal academics that were obviously part of that Eastern Cape political subset that the ANC was extremely active in that part of the world. It's the part of the world where Nelson Mandela's original traditional Xhosa village is, and where Mandela Bay is today.

At Rhodes we had a very interesting mix of people. Many of the Rhodesian, ex-Rhodesian or white Rhodesian students favoured Rhodes as a university town. We had boys that had just come out of the military who were trying to get an education, we had guys that had just come out of school there and had seen the change that had happened, families being ruined by war, and obviously a big change in politics. There were also exiles that had had to leave Rhodesia, or Zimbabwe as it is now known, and come to South Africa.

Among these students were obviously the white South African students who were schooled in a political mainstream educational environment, brought up to fear the "Swart Gevaar" or "Black Danger" and black governments. Now we were all mixing in a liberal academic environment where that was not the message we were hearing and certainly not experiencing. For the first time we were on campus with some black, coloured and Indian students, and Rhodes had really taken some tremendous early steps in transformation. I'm certainly proud of that as an Alumnus. I think my political awakening really came from seeing protesting students. The SRC were protesting certain policies, and I became aware that there were other voices and other reasons to live in South Africa. My own political background was shaped by a fairly liberal PFP supporting family, my Christian family with the Christian and of course the Jewish background. I suppose the Jews were very close to struggle politics, being a persecuted nation, and of course some of that came through from my family background.

I became very good friends with a lady with whom we shared a house, Toni Petra, and she was the other influencing factor that I had. Toni was deeply involved in PFP activities and was head of the PFP Youth League on campus in the Eastern Cape. She shared her understanding of liberal politics and democracy, and what fairness and equal votes and human rights were all about. I must say I got deeply involved in conversations and took to heart the plight of people who did not have the vote and didn't have equal human rights. From the early days I really supported the struggle in several different ways. We had our house under police surveillance all the time because of Toni's presence there.

Our house that we moved into in our third year was right on the edge of the Township called Fingo Village, and in Number 2 York Street we had very close access to the township. We used to have military Casspirs parked outside our house and during the tough days, the really tough days, they used to mount a massive aerial spotlight on top of the Monument Hill. This would shine down into the township so that troops on the grounds could see what was going on in some of the township areas and coordinate added security for the forces to keep a check on activities in the township. Township politics became really nasty, there were boycotts on white shops, and anybody that broke the boycott was viciously dealt with to the extent that some people used to get necklaced. This was a horrible practice where a tyre used to be squashed over the head and arms of a victim, petrol was poured into the tyre rim and all over the individual, and the individual was set alight like a human torch. This was the cruellest and most brutal way of dealing with dissidents against the revolution, but the revolution was coming, there was no way of stopping it. Unfortunately, the ANC struggle had to resort to those types of tactics, it was cruel and nasty and I really couldn't ever condone that, but politics was rough. Grahamstown police were brutal as well, I remember getting sjamboked and tear-gassed at a student rally that we participated in on the lawns of the university and it was a tough scene. There were campus spies – books have been written about that - and we were certainly watched, controlled and I suppose feared by the South African Police, but their brutality certainly injected enough fear in everybody else to keep us in some sort of reasonable check. I remember one festival we used to have on one of the campus social and drinking areas, police threw a teargas canister into the midst of these students, and hundreds of students started to panic and run and flee and scramble and trample each other and it was a miracle that nobody actually got killed in that stampede. It was a very, very scary thing and it created a great deal of anger within the student body. All in all, the politics at Rhodes taught me a great deal. It was an educational time, it was academic, and it was a good balanced view in a very unbalanced society.

Eight

Rhodes; the Music and the Studies

"Where words fail, music speaks." – Hans Christian Andersen

MUSIC CAN BE A big influencing factor on anybody's life, and it was definitely a big influence on mine at the time of moving to university. Although I was not a big music aficionado, I certainly loved listening to good music, I loved dancing, and pretty much enjoyed many good tunes, but looking back on those times, the influence of music was certainly quite powerful. In those days of course, Sun City was the only place really bringing in international artists, through Sol Kerzner's international connections. Most musicians boycotted coming to tour in South Africa so they went to Sun City in the old homeland of Bophuthatswana. I remember my friend Rob Smuts and a couple of guys driving in his Datsun 120Y all the way up to Sun City. We left on a Friday, got there on Saturday, watched the show on Saturday night and drove all the way back on Sunday – it was crazy as it was 14 hours from Grahamstown up to Sun City! It was almost unimaginable, but we did it as the passion for the music was there. That time we had travelled up to see Queen, and it was well worth the trip.

We also had the odd South African band on campus. Bands like Evoid and Juluka were huge outfits at the time, Mango Groove was also on the scene. I loved Evoid, I loved the Ndebele beads they wore, I loved the African fusion and certainly for me Juluka was a favourite band and we saw them many times. Their music and the lyrics are also encouraging a different way of thinking of our African heritage, our Zulu heritage in South Africa and being sensitive to another culture. Of course, Rodriguez and his unbelievable music like Sugarman, and all of those songs that were so famous in South Africa but unheard of elsewhere in the world, this was a kind of revolutionary music as well. The romantic tunes of Michael Franks and Kenny G were incredible music which I recount and remember personally. Then there was my love for Bob Marley and Eddie Grant and the reggae tunes pulling through from my school days.

I was influenced by some of the books that I read as part of my extra curriculum. I was introduced to the writings of Khalil Gibran the Prophet, by a girlfriend who was doing her masters in linguistics or something like that. She was quite a wild chic from the UK but she introduced me to these amazing writings. I read a book by Og Mandino called "The World's Greatest Salesman", that my dad gave me. That had a huge impact on me in terms of being a business book but also a book of deep philosophy and yearning for greatness and riches. The other aspect of reading and coming in touch with so many different schools of thought was especially inspired in my study of psychology. I was exposed to some interesting leading clinical psychologists at the Rhodes Psychology Department. I had the privilege of doing a course with Professor Dreyer Kruger, and it was really a course on what he called Phenomenology and how memory is embedded in things other than just your mind. Today I still find it so relevant in terms of looking at the world from a different perspective. I am so grateful for my studies in psychology and the understanding of the human mind and behavioural psychology, for being exposed to the great minds and thinkers, such as Freud and Skinner and many other great psychologists of the world.

My combination of psychology with business studies such as economics and law also provided a wonderful kind of counter- intuitive thinking process. It was one of world economics, macro and microeconomics, and

I really loved that. Together with law and practical things like accounting and business administration, these really gave me what I thought was a wonderful exposure to different ways of thinking. I am so pleased for that, even though it wasn't a classical B Comm and I struggled greatly with accounting, but it gave me a nice, well-rounded experience but nothing that really qualified me to do anything.

Nine

The Experiences and the Drama

"There was never yet an uninteresting life. Such a thing is an impossibility. Inside of the dullest exterior, there is a drama, a comedy, and a tragedy." - Mark Twain

I WANT TO TELL a little story about Mountain Drive. Mountain Drive was at the back of our residence and it was a forested hill, with some legends around witchcraft and weird things happening up there. We found it to be a magnificent sunrise drinking spot and I say sunrise because normally when the pubs closed down at midnight, we'd go and raid our local pub in the hostel or in our residence, grab a case of beers and head up for Mountain Drive and drink until the sun came up in the morning. Many, many wonderful tales were told up there and plenty of nonsense but more than that, great friendships were formed. We were talking and talking until the sun came up, sharing our thoughts and ideas, jokes, laughter and fun, overlooking the valley of Grahamstown with the twinkling lights. It was one of the incredible experiences at Rhodes University.

The drama happened one evening when a friend, in a rather hammered state, tried opening a beer bottle with another bottle, a technique that is quite simple and effective if you don't have a bottle opener. Something went horribly wrong and the neck of one of the bottles broke open and he pushed that broken glass into his other hand, nearly slicing off his entire thumb.

It's at moments like this that as a young man I realised living this crazy hedonistic life there was always someone or something looking out for us.

I was a highly trained first aider through my scouting experience and I have always had this ability to kick into top gear when there is a crisis and all the adrenaline sobered me up faster than I could imagine. I quickly stopped the massive bleeding and bandaged up the hand with strips of a tee shirt that I had to tear up and got him to the hospital where the doctors were able to save his thumb.

Ten

Drinking Clubs

"Drink never made a man better, but it made many a man think he was better." - Finley Peter Dunne

THE DRINKING CLUBS AT Rhodes University were rather notorious clubs and I think they might finally have been banned. There were many of these different drinking clubs and you had to get invited to attend a drinking club. Then there was a whole series of initiations and on club days, some of the guys would wear their suits with their badges and they all had different names and it was quite a scene. Anyway, I didn't ever crack the nod to get involved in a drinking club and I was quite happy about that in one way but sad in another. At Rhodes there were really two strong groups of students. The first were called the Buggers or the drinking club hardened. They were the sports loving macho kind of clan, together with all their groupies. This included the young wannabe-marry-the-rugby-captain type of girls, maybe even themselves sports stars, netball, tennis or whatever, into that whole sporting space or mindset.

On the other hand there was the sort of hippie era student, which included the art students, the drama students, the journalism students, really all the "hey man, let's be cool and have some dope, let's get wasted, let's talk philosophy and politics and all sorts of things" group. Those were called the Bungees. So those were the groups - the Buggers and the Bungees - and I never really fell into either camp but I sort of migrated between the different camps. I often thought "I wonder if I am just enjoying the best of both worlds and having great fun, or do I have a kind of a personality confusion as to where I want to be?" Truth be told,

I didn't want to be classified in any group of students, and nor do I want to have that classification as an individual and human being even now. I am a unique person. I can associate with different people, with diverse cultures and in a wide variety of settings and feel comfortable in any one of these environments, obviously environments that I deem to be healthy and respectful. But the Bungees and the Buggers were two definite environments, I loved partying in both areas and of course at Rhodes there was always alcohol, or a bit of the green stuff involved, or both – a lot of the time both, and it was great fun.

Eleven

Near Death

"Sometimes a little near death experience helps them put things into perspective." - Anne Shrops hire

BEING AT RHODES THERE was also always the odd tragedy, student deaths by road accidents or things like that, illness, suffering, and it was always very sad, but somehow it was always out there, it was far away and never close at hand. This was until I had my own weird, near death experience.

We were out partying one night; I didn't feel well, and the guys thought I maybe had too much to drink or something wrong to eat. I left the party thinking "This is not good. I'm going to make my way home." I went home and went straight to bed. I woke up the next morning, still not feeling very good at all, but I walked down to get something to eat, and by the time I came back I really, really wasn't well. I felt terrible in fact and when I looked in the mirror, I had this haemorrhaging under my skin. Somebody took me off to the university sanatorium where they took one look at me and isolated me. I think I must have had several seizures during that time. I had a high fever too and I got rushed down to a hospital in Port Elizabeth where I finally came around. My mother and father had been requested to fly down and basically say goodbye to me because I had contracted what they thought was Congo Fever, something that had killed several students and people in the Eastern Cape area. It was caused by a little tick from a bird… Anyway, how I got this thing I don't know, maybe it was on one of my trips up Mountain Drive, but it was very, very worrying. When I saw my parents, I got a shock, thinking "whoah, what are you doing here?" They tried to keep themselves together, and I can't imagine what that must have been like for them, but the long and the short of it is that I didn't succumb to the illness. I did get better and it must have been the answer to many, many prayers at the time but it really set me back quite a bit academically as I had missed a few weeks. Despite this I managed to gather myself for the final exams. I wrote the exams and amazingly passed a few subjects, enough to get back for my third year at Rhodes. But I think that experience did change me quite a bit. It helped me get more serious about my studying, and I even became somewhat more appreciative of the life I had been afforded and matters of my health.

Twelve

York Street

"It is penance to work, to give oneself to others, to endure the pinpricks of community living." - Dorothy Day

THIRD YEAR SAW ME enter digs, and digs is really a residential house which students rented, for the year. Rob and I had resolved to stay together. Gordon was a friend of ours we had come into contact with, and he needed a place to stay and was looking for a digs so he planned to join us. Gordon was also studying a BComm but with business and science, information science or information technology or whatever it was called then, and so Gordon and I got together in Jo'burg – his mother was very concerned about how we were going to cope, just the three boys together. Anyway, we got kitted out with kitchen equipment and all sorts of things, we rented this funny little house called 2 York Street, and York Street had two famous res's. Well one was famous, and one was ours and famous for us. The York Street Digs was an absolute hellhole of a place to live, I don't know who actually lived there, but it was predominantly Zimbabwean or Rhodesian students. They used to have the wildest drinking parties almost every weekend and you could go there and get absolutely hammered. There was always something on the go and it had a reputation of being a bit of a dog show. Our res or our digs was on the opposite corner of York Street, just behind the filling station, very close to the main road and of course to the main township at the end of Grahamstown. It was an interesting 1820 settlers' house, the walls were about a metre thick, the floorboards were wooden, the roof was made of zinc or tin, and it was a funny little house. But we got stuck into it, we painted it, we freshened it up, put in new carpets and new curtains and turned it into a really lekker little digs. Unfortunately Rob went back to university to write a few supplementary exams and he didn't pass his final sup, so he headed back to complete his degree through UNISA and start working - so that was exit Rob and we needed to find someone to come into res with us. That was when Andrew Crawford from Cape Town joined us. He was a real private school wally, from a family with too much money. He was a bit of a weird guy, but that was some more fun in York Street!

I must admit that having to run your own home, do all the washing, cooking and ironing, make beds, look after yourself, and remember to lock up the house, that was certainly a growing up period and we learnt fast. We learnt how to budget, to plan and to get by. This gave us a tremendous sense of achievement and of achieving independence and in a way, manhood, where we were men who could look after each other or ourselves. The cars were another point of interest. Gordon had a silver XR3 that he would zoom around in and it was a very cool student car. I pranged my little Golf and came back in this Ford Cortina that was called the Free State Ferrari. It was baby blue in colour and went like the clappers with its 2L engine. It was a really cool car for me, and I loved it! Anyway, that was York Street, plenty of fun, good parties, and many memories made in that house.

Thirteen

Port Alfred

"Live in the sunshine, swim in the sea, drink the wild air."
– Ralph Waldo Emerson

THE EASTERN CAPE GROWS on you slowly, and Grahamstown was certainly a variable place in terms of its weather – you could have all four seasons in one day. Winter was horrendously cold, so much so that we used to have ice on the roads, and we had to be very careful going home. But it also could be hot as hell in summer, there was high humidity and everything in between. Grahamstown on a wet, grey, misty day is quite a romantic place to be. I suppose you get used to all of its facets and its weather, its beautiful historic buildings, its truly beautiful campus, Rhodes University, and the little town and its pubs: The Vic, Stonies and The Cockhouse and all sorts of places – it really was a delightful, charming university town to enjoy.

But one of the other wonderful things about the Eastern Cape was its coastline, Port Alfred, Kenton, East London, Port Elizabeth, and everything in between there, as well as further afield into the Transkei and places like Hole in the Wall which is a beautiful, beautiful place along the coast. We were very privileged; a friend of mine's father was a powerful legal eagle and he had this massive house built in Port Alfred. We used to nip down there and enjoy this house or holiday home – spend the weekend there, drink copious amounts of alcohol and spend long days on the beach. I was also involved in windsurfing, and we used to take our windsurfers down to the coast, where we'd also try our hand at a bit of paddle skiing, surfing, boogie boarding and body surfing - you name it, we did it. It involved beaches, fun, sun, women, alcohol, good times, braaiing, just the idyllic South African life and lifestyle. It was a 35 – 40 minute drive to Port Alfred, Kenton and Bushman's River, all absolutely stunning places to sail and to enjoy. We certainly did that on many great occasions.

Steve's dad had this huge deep-sea fishing boat in the garage but when they were down there they'd moor it in the river. They had this little tender boat that was a little tiny thing, with a small Seagull engine on it to ferry between the wharf and the moored deep sea fishing boat. One thing I really loved was the excursions on the tender boat. We used this boat to go up the river to go crab fishing, we'd go quite a way up the river at Port Alfred, with this little putt-putt engine. We'd prepare orange sacks full of last night's braai bones and bits and pieces and sometimes we'd buy some fish heads and things from the local bait shop and we would head up the river. These sacks would be weighted down and there would be a net around it, and we'd drop these nets down to the riverbed where hopefully we'd attract the scavenger crabs on the bottom, particularly on the river bends. Then when we'd pull it up, and if we were lucky enough to have caught anything we'd have the difficult task of getting these massive crabs into a bucket with a lid on the top of it, in this small tinny boat. Many times a crab got loose and started slashing away with its giant pincers and guys would bail out of the boat! But after order was restored we would then take these huge crabs that we caught in the river home with us and boil them up. These dark muddy looking river crabs turned into this bright pinky-red cooked crab and it made the most delicious meal you can imagine. It was like lobster and caviar for a student. Whenever we got a couple of crabs it was a feast of feasts! Of course, being able to catch it was free, and sometimes that was all we had – so we might be relying on our crab catch, and when we didn't catch anything it was bitterly disappointing. But many days of fun were had, just going up the river, enjoying the experience while smoking and drinking and talking nonsense and catching crabs. I can honestly say we had a wonderful time on so many evenings on that little tender boat.

Fourteen
How School Friends Faded

"True friendship can afford true knowledge. It does not depend on darkness and ignorance." - Henry David Thoreau

BEING AT RHODES EVERY year meant spending another year away from my school mates. Some of them I stayed in touch with, but very slowly those relationships faded. My life took a significant turn; I like to think for the better, as I was growing, learning, maturing, taking on new things and meeting people from different backgrounds. I was really growing up as a young man and understanding my own identity in the world – after that my school friends faded quite rapidly. Every now and again, when I was coming back to Johannesburg and meeting up with them, it wasn't quite the same. They'd also taken different paths and some of my school friends did join me at Rhodes – Steven Burrell joined us a year or two later. My friend Mark Shannahan, from early days in my schooling, also came down to Rhodes. Although we saw each other and were friendly, he was staying in another res, so he developed different friends and we grew apart. I think there's a certain sadness and a joy in moving on and maturing and growing but I was always mindful of that because I am a tremendously loyal person. I like to believe my relationships endure as long-term relationships. That's just the kind of person I am.

• • • • • • • • • •

After my third year, I had done relatively well, I had passed all my subjects and it was on to the final year – I had three majors in my final year and one first year credit to pick up, which I did successfully. I must say I loved every minute of Rhodes, the memories that I made there, as well as the friends that are now lifetime friends. I certainly would recommend my old alumni as a wonderful place to study and would recommend a small-town environment over the big cities. That campus experience is so rich in so many ways other than just the academics. The academics are good too, but if I look around at successful Rhodes University students, of which there are many, I think it's the complete education, the holistic education, that makes the biggest difference. It's about growing people, both young men and women, giving them space to find out who they are, to meet new friends, to study, to play sport, to grow and to develop. Obviously, many students drop out, but those that stay and pass the test and graduate do come out as well-rounded individuals.

I hit the books hard and after spending 4 years at Rhodes University, I finally completed a Bachelor of Commerce majoring in Economics, Commercial Law and Clinical Psychology. I really was very proud of being able to graduate and the graduation ceremony at Rhodes was something special – I didn't think I'd feel as excited and alive to the possibilities of life on that particular day as I did. It was a huge moment for me.

Fifteen

Job Seeking and a Corporate Career

"If opportunity doesn't knock, build a door." – Milton Berle

By THE END OF my time at Rhodes University, I was ready for the Big Smoke. I couldn't wait to get back home, get out of the small town of Grahamstown, and get back to what I thought was the real world, and to start making a career and forging forward. It was time to go and find a job and make some money and prove to the world that I'd learned something along the way.

My graduation had been a tremendously proud moment for me, and I suppose that's what made the next 6 months the toughest. My head was full of great ideas, full of wonderful learnings, and I had dreams and aspirations to fulfil, but now followed the hard task of finding a job. I wasn't one of those bursary degree guys that could walk straight into a job so I had to hit the job market like everybody else, which was quite tough I must say. After several interviews with agencies, putting my CV out everywhere and quite a few disappointments along the way, it was getting to the stage after about a 6-month period where I was really feeling quite down about not having a job yet. I can certainly relate and sympathise with all of those young people who are coming out with good qualifications and degrees today that are just not finding jobs, either because of the tough economic situation, or because corporates really are not that receptive to hiring college or university graduates with little or no experience. I suppose that's also why I have gotten involved with this and created a non-profit organisation for youth employment.

• • • • ● • ● • • •

Anglo

Anyway, I finally did get a job. I landed a kind of apprentice management training programme in the mining industry with Anglo American Gold Division. Of course, this certainly wasn't my dream job and it was an industry sector that I didn't have an affinity to, but it was a huge sector of the economy. South Africa is very famous for its commodity markets, gold being top of that pile. Certainly, for the career path that I wanted to explore, being labour and industrial relations, it gave me the foot in the door that I needed. So I packed up and went to work in Carletonville. Now Carletonville is a small mining town, about an hour's drive outside of Johannesburg, right in the mining belt of South Africa. That mine, Western Deep Levels, was known as one of the deepest mines in the world, with multiple shafts going down, down, down and even further down into the earth. At the time I think it employed in excess of thirty thousand mining personnel, all working multiple shifts and around the clock. To say it was a conservative Afrikaans dominated industry would be an understatement; it certainly was a far cry from the liberal free-thinking environment that I had just graduated from. But nonetheless it was a job, it had a training programme and I just got on with it. The kind of programme that I entered involved spending a couple of weeks in each department of the mine. This started with the time office and the pay office, going through various parts of the HR supply chain, and really getting experience and exposure to all the different aspects. One of the things that really stood out for me was the time I had to do my two- or three-week stint in the mine hostel. The hostel housed only black workers and there were only men employed at the time. It was run a bit like a prison camp where these guys would sleep in men's quarters, with many, many different nationalities together. Even at that time, migrant labour from Mozambique, Angola and Namibia were all part of that make up. Anyway, I got quite involved in administration, and it was quite an experience, and I even participated in the hostel's One Mile race, which was a big thing in itself.

The mining hostel was a huge environment where I think they slept up to fifteen thousand people in one hostel. We got involved with the catering department too – we got exposed to the kitchens and all sorts of things where cooking meals for that number of people was amazing. There were five thousand people per shift or something like that. The first time I've ever seen a production kitchen that huge, making mielie pap in almost a silo to feed the guys, it was a real eye opener. Security was very high in these environments because they were known to be hotbeds of trouble. Unions obviously had a lot of control, there was factionalism between the different tribal groupings and it really was a microcosm, it was a boiling pot that was South Africa at that time.

The lifestyle of these men that worked all day from the early morning till the afternoon was very intense. They would come in, hundreds of them at a time, and all get showered up and then hit the pub where they'd have a big jug of local Mageu beer. Next they would have their meal and obviously their evening sleep before the next shift. It was a very dense social concentration of human power and energy, and you certainly could feel that during that time.

A huge thing for the mine's communities was safety of personnel. They used to count the number of man hours as an indicator of accident free, or fatality free, and the big milestone was to hit one million man hours without a fatality. Now that seems a huge amount of man hours but on a mine that size it was achievable in four or five months. Unfortunately, being deep level mining, fatalities were a part of the equation as it is a very dangerous mining environment. That got even more dangerous when guys flaunted the safety procedures and requirements, so there was a big focus on compliance to safety and health regulations. Nonetheless, with mining at that level, when the earth moves, or there's seismic activity, it's very easy for people to get crushed and trapped under the rock. In the one year that I was there, involved in that shaft, I think we had a total of something like 12 or 14 fatalities which was a horrendous statistic, and I wasn't comfortable working in that kind of environment.

We did however achieve, during a three or four month period, a million man hours fatality free. I hadn't known but there was an incentive in place, that if the mine achieved that target, they would throw a huge big braai and a party to celebrate that. Anyway, a funny story came out of this party involving one of my older colleagues who was a bit of a rogue and a serious drinker. In fact, everybody was a serious drinker at that time, and he shall remain nameless, but he was one of the Human Resource guys. He was much more senior than I was and he took a liking to this little English guy that he found quite strange, but he still took me under his wing. At this party he got so inebriated he eventually drove home with what he thought were the spoils of the party. He thought he had found a whole box of meat and braaipacks, and he was going to take that home, put it in his deep freeze and dine out on that for the next couple of weeks. In his drunken state, he didn't take home a box of meat at all, but rather a huge box of firelighters! He promptly put it in his freezer, and his wife had an argument with him and said, "We're not putting that in the deep freeze!" He argued, eventually won the argument and then passed out in bed. The next morning she said to him "Listen, I think you need to go and remove the firelighters from the deep freeze", and he again argued about it being plenty of meat, but of course she proved him wrong when he opened the freezer and there was this big box of firelighters squashed in there. It became quite the standing joke amongst all the Human Resource guys and one of the things that I have remembered to this day.

· · · ● · ● · ● · ● · ·

But apart from the moments like that, I couldn't get out of there fast enough, and once I had ticked off all my training programmes, I was back on the job market. One of the other things that we used to do on a regular basis was go through to a town called Welkom, where they had the centralised training facility where we would go and study modules and so on. I was friendly with a guy by the name of Sammy, one of the black graduates who were part of the programme, one of the very few black graduates that got into mining, also in the HR environment, and he was a character of note. He was quite a womaniser and he always used to get very lucky with the ladies. We used to stay in the Holiday Inn down in Welkom, and the hotel had a loyalty programme. For every night's stay that you were there, they'd give you a little sort of smiley face stamp on a card that you collected, and once you had filled up the card, I think it was after twenty nights, you'd get one night free. Anyway, Sammy would try to bend the rules and his local girlfriend at the Holiday Inn reception was more than happy to fill up a card or two just to see him smile. So Sammy and I collected a couple of these cards and I later used them for a boys' weekend down in Durban, but it was one of my early exposures to loyalty cards and what to do and not do in running a programme! But all in all, that was again plenty of fun and I look upon those times with AngloGold Mining with great fondness.

Welkom

One of the other stories and memories about my days at Anglo, when we were in Welkom, was this fantastic little steakhouse in the heart of Welkom. It was very near the Hofie, which was a place where guys used to go Boulevard cruising with their souped-up Toyota Corollas and all sorts of fancy cars. Eagles Restaurant was owned by a guy by the name of Gerrie and he served a fantastic steak. We used to go in there whenever we could, and we really got to be good friends with him. Later on, I reconnected with Gerrie, he owned and ran a very, very successful restaurant called Browns in Rivonia, Johannesburg. Browns became a great regular meeting place and venue for fine dining and good wine drinking – Gerrie always had a superb selection of wines. Later on he opened a restaurant in London with his business partner, and on one of my visits to London later on I met up with him. Gerrie had shipped all his South African wines across, bottle by bottle, and of course that was his working capital or near enough, that then allowed him to start up that business in the UK. I'm sure Gerrie is still doing very well, he provided one of the finest examples of customer service in the restaurant industry, and Gerrie's story is a good one. I look back with fondness on the many nights we enjoyed at Eagles.

· • • •· • •· • · ·

One of the other interesting stories I had at Anglo American, in the mining division, was that NUM, the National Union of Mine Workers, was at the time led and headed by Cyril Ramaphosa, now President of South Africa. Cyril was a very powerful negotiator and on the Anglo side was the venerable Bobbie Godsell, who was head of labour relations. He was also a visionary thinker in terms of employment equity, employment law, and was probably responsible for a big chunk of what we now know as our Labour Law in the new democratic South Africa. Clem Sunter was also a strategic decision maker with him at Anglo Gold business and obviously a man with a big vision. With the two of them behind it, Anglo became the first business in South Africa to offer an employee equity incentive scheme for black workers at every level in the business. This was a result of one of the major trade union negotiations that took place. I was certainly very proud to work for a company at the time that was ahead of its game; that had bridged the gap by offering workers an equity stake in the mineral wealth of South Africa, a country where those players certainly believed everybody was entitled to a share of its national wealth. I think Anglo set the tone for other equity shareholder schemes and today as we see with the BEE codes, this was a very popular way of bringing large groups of employees into equity and ownership of a company, in a transformation agenda. Incredible that this started way back in the day when I was a junior or trainee HR manager almost thirty years ago.

Barlows

As much as I was very grateful to Anglo American for giving me a foot into the job market, I couldn't wait to get out of the mining environment. I found it extremely tough and conservative, very Afrikaans and very oppressive from a labour perspective. I certainly didn't like it and I didn't really get into it in a big way. I had a look at a couple of positions, and I was approached by a Human Resource manager at Barlows Caterpillar and Earth Moving manufacturing company. I went for some interviews and I got the job. This was at a big production facility in Boksburg on the East Rand of Johannesburg, about a 25-30-minute drive from my parents' home in Sandton. I also couldn't wait to get out of single's quarters in Anglo, which was where all the non-married guys used to stay in something like a big hostel. There were some horrendous things that used to go on there. So I was happy to be back in Jo'burg, and I could then look at renting a small place for myself, and getting settled down a little bit better. Barlows was a big conglomerate of a company, and its Caterpillar Earth Moving Equipment division had the licence to sell Caterpillar products in Africa, and in South Africa, as well as to manufacture some of the product lines. I ended up working in a factory that built huge truck bodies and the big dozer blades and graders that graded and flattened the surfaces of roads and road developments. The hydraulic componentry and many of the parts were also made or assembled and then mounted on the engine. It was a big factory, employing two and a half thousand people, and the predominant union was the Metal Workers Union of South Africa, NUMSA, which is also a very big part of the COSATU coalition. It was quite a difference in industry, hopping from mining to manufacturing, or metal working specifically, and I really enjoyed the change. I loved the process of manufacturing where you could see the product coming in as raw material, being laser cut, shaped and fashioned together, then put into these massive jigs to be welded or ground down, shotblasted, painted and then finally assembled. I loved the process of taking something from scratch and building it up; and I suppose that's also my passion for start-ups in the entrepreneurial space. I really love seeing something come from nothing, being built up and nurtured into something that can have great value.

I started at Barlows as a Human Resources Officer, and I underwent a very good induction programme where I got to understand all the various different aspects of this particular business. Then my boss was fired for fiddling with the books or something like that. Apparently, he was recruiting people, charging the business recruiting fees and then basically paying himself which was unethical and illegal, so he got fired for that, which left a vacancy. I applied for the vacancy and was turned down because I was too young as a junior for the top role as Human Resource director or manager. A new guy was brought in who turned out to be a phenomenal boss; and Rob France is still a friend today. He's an incredible man, absolutely cut out for the human resource and human sciences side of things. He still remembers my birthday to this day, and phones me every year to wish me well. Rob was a gentle but firm man and had good HR experience. He gave me opportunities to grow as well, and I headed up Industrial Relations and training, which was a new thing for me and I really enjoyed that. I enjoyed running the apprenticeship programme for young boilermakers, welders, fitters and turners coming into the business. We would take them through our own initiative programme, link them up to a senior to give mentorship, coaching and training and watch them grow. That training was a very rewarding experience for me and I am still very passionate about this training, coaching and mentoring aspect of business in general. It led to a later start-up of a training business called The Performance Academy that held the Ken Blanchard franchise for leadership development in South Africa.

In my tenure with Barlows, which was about 5 years, the manufacturing organisation went through a huge change. It changed its basic method of production to a production methodology called Just in Time. This was derived from Japanese efficiency where parts and equipment are manufactured just in time to arrive at the assembly line, just in time to be assembled, thereby avoiding pulling items from a stock register from huge amounts of stock in a massive stock room. This meant the business could thin out its investment in stock in trade. Obviously to get this "Just in Time" process working, one has to re-engineer every aspect of the business, including suppliers and processors and how you move parts around a big factory. Naturally it also slims down on some personnel, more specifically warehouse personnel, and it makes the business much leaner. It was a rather traumatic process for the business because this was a manufacturing business that had been in existence for many, many years, decades even, but it needed to go through this change and adjustment to produce better results financially. We hired a very senior engineer who wasn't very well liked, but he was my pick for the job. He then gathered a team around him that was from all the different disciplines of the business, including myself from Human Resources. Our department was then responsible for the human sciences side of things, for change management and training, re-training and so on, in fact all the change management dynamics.

The result of this process was fairly painful in that we had to conduct a first round of retrenchments, and we slimmed down the business by almost three or four hundred people. That was a painful process for me personally. We thought it was all over and that we had succeeded in the project, but unfortunately what followed next was Caterpillar America's decision to pull back some of its product lines to manufacture further in the United States. This was part of the political sanctions that the world was putting on South Africa. Caterpillar came under much stress to disinvest from South Africa, in order to put political pressure on the then National Party to change. This then resulted in a huge loss of jobs at our production factory, and we had to cut a further seven or eight hundred jobs. We basically went from two and a half thousand employees like there had been when I started there, to slightly less than a thousand, and it was a very, very difficult thing to do. This awful process ultimately resulted in my complete disillusionment with the corporate world and how it worked, but that was also the very early seeding of my desire to do something different, and to make a difference too.

Within my time at Barlows I obviously built up an extremely good relationship with the trade unions as that was my key performance area. We would meet regularly, with the shop stewards and workers. We all had a good working relationship, but it was certainly no pushover relationship as they were hard on us. We went through several years of tough wage negotiations where I learnt a huge amount on both the wage negotiations and negotiations in general. I did a phenomenal course at a business school one year, relating to negotiations. It was of great value and I use some of the things I learnt from that course still today. But when it came down to this final round of retrenchments, it really broke my heart to have to do this to people with whom I had built up a five-year working relationship with, established trust and mutual respect. As a business we were also a leader in the field, instrumental in doing positive things, practising corporate social responsibility for our workforce in the areas that they lived, and the township of Daveyton was one of those areas. I was instrumental in taking many of our products, graders and dozers, into the township to clear and grade fields, and upgrade soccer and athletics fields for recreational purposes. We did charity work and we had really established a phenomenal relationship with our workforce which I think was way ahead of its time and its thinking. So yet again there was this tremendous trauma and tension in my heart about what needed to be done in terms of retrenching so many people.

Barlows was also a working environment where I learnt so much about leadership and how not to practice it. This particular environment was very engineering oriented, and Barlows itself was a serious accounting oriented leadership structure, where it was all about the money and how many beans you made at the end of the day. To be quite honest, the leadership that I saw there was totally uninspiring, and I was sadly disappointed to see how managers were so often looking after their own interests, not looking at the interests of the greater good. They were totally one dimensional in their performance focus around bottom line profitability, and not looking at what we now know today as the triple bottom line. We had this tension between the Afrikaans conservative or racist type of managerial behaviour and the more liberal English-speaking managers, where people of colour and different cultures were not a factor. In the workplace in those days it was frequently "them and us" in terms of the workers, the black workers and their mentality, and the prejudices that people had. It was the scare factor that the government had successfully been able to create through propaganda, what was known as the "Swart Gevaar". People were told to be careful of this potential danger, of the blacks becoming too powerful, taking over and bringing chaos and so on. That was really the way so many people in South Africa lived at the time. They didn't know any better and that thinking pattern was continually drummed and brainwashed into the populace by the government of the time, the National Party.

When you work with people, and you get to know them, their families, their dreams, their aspirations for their children and their children's schooling, it's hard not to break out of that kind of thinking. But there were some people who desperately wanted to cling on to it, and they themselves became propaganda puppets for that way of thinking. It was also during that time that I read my first Ken Blanchard book which was called "Gung Ho". It was about a factory that transformed through the engagement of their employees and how their employees made a difference. I was convinced that instead of cutting back our workforce and going that hard-core route, the right way of doing it would be to have engaged with our workforce to find alternative solutions, to find a way of bringing life and profit and sustainability into our factories – but my voice was a very small voice in a very crowded room, being drowned out by cost-cutters and engineers who eventually won the day and the argument. The result was that several hundred people had to be retrenched, and of course I was the "axe" that had to tell the trade unions, and physically go through all of the retrenchment discussions. It was in many of those discussions I had with individuals that grown men would break down into tears and beg me not to put them on the list. They would beg me for a job because their child's future was at stake, and as a young twenty-eight-year-old, the pressure was far more than I could bear, and the personal heartache was outrageous. Even now I am emotional telling this part of the story because it really broke my heart to do this, and I was so in conflict with what was being done. I felt that I was on the wrong team, doing the wrong thing and this was totally against my values, and that I should be on the trade union team, fighting for the rights of workers and not compromising my values. It was really hard and this internal struggle continued to the point where I knew that I needed to go as well.

Sixteen

First Steps and Catalysts

"Success is not final; failure is not fatal: it is the courage
to continue that counts." – Winston Churchill

I SUPPOSE LIKE MANY things, making a decision or move of that kind of
significance, some stars had certainly aligned for me. I had really got to a
stage in my own job where I believed that I needed to make the next move,
I had grown significantly, I had learnt a great deal but now it was time. The
trade union situation at Barlow Equipment Manufacturing Company was
at the lowest ebb ever, it had become quite aggressive. Many, many people
had been retrenched, and I was certainly feeling very down about this, so
much so that my gym friend at the Health and Racket Club in Sandton
said to me one day, "Dave, why are you so down, what's going on in your
life?" After some reflection I had to tell him that I was no longer loving
my job, I certainly didn't love going to work with the prospect of running
another disciplinary enquiry, or to fire somebody for stealing something
small, when I knew that the Managing Director was stealing the time of
the maintenance department to fix his Pretoria home, on top of which he
was stealing company assets. There were many other things that were just
not right. I hated the fact that we had to retrench people and impact lives,
of not only that person, but that person's wife, children, possibly parents
that he or she was supporting. The whole community was dying because of
a nasty situation that I believe our business leaders should have been able to
resolve but weren't trying to do. Our political climate was such that there
was tension between the working classes that were majority black, coloured
and Indian, who didn't have the vote in our country, and this was also a

catalyst. I was sick and tired of that, I was part of the liberal mindset and consciousness in South Africa that said it was enough now – the old ways were the wrong ways – and that we needed change.

The final straw for me was when I was driving out of the factory one day; I had encountered some pretty dangerous union activity that could have led to an extremely ugly situation. I felt my life was in danger and luckily I was able to speed away from the incident and run home, with tears in my eyes, for these were the same people I had so much respect for. I knew that they were doing this out of tremendous frustration and a desperate attempt to be heard. So I came to work the following day and I said to my boss that I would like to be retrenched as well; and that I wanted to use the money that I get from my retrenchment to start a small business. My boss Rob was very gracious, he negotiated an exit plan for me with the managing director of that business, and I was able, along with all those other workers, to leave the company and have a little bit of money in my back pocket to start something new. I was also very fortunate, because at that time I met a young man who became a very dear friend of mine and with whom I eventually started the Uwin Iwin business.

This was the other wonderful thing that happened that was a catalyst. I met two guys who were entrepreneurs, they were young guys that had been well educated and had already made the move into "Let's build something, let's do something for ourselves, rather than work for shareholders and bosses", and so those were the kinds of catalysts that helped me make the decision to move.

· · · ●·● ·· ·

Here followed the first steps of my entrepreneurial journey. I had spent about seven years post-university making a career in the giant corporate world of South Africa. The first two companies were certainly as Blue Chip as they get – Anglo American and Barlows, or what is now Barlow World. In some ways I was very proud of my early achievements but in other ways I knew deep down in my soul that I didn't want to work in that corporate environment, making a career as a corporate citizen, working my way up the ranks towards a senior managerial level, ultimately a board position in one of these great giant corporates. I was fuelled also by the passion to do something meaningful. I wanted to change the world of work where people, no matter what shift they may be working on, could engage and be in an environment that was stimulating, exciting, and a happy place to be. I wanted their efforts to be met with meaningful rewards. I didn't see that happening in corporate life. I saw people coming from day to day, rather numbed by their experience of life, living out a mediocre existence, not really that enthusiastic, not really bringing their passion and energy and "A" game to the table. Certainly, corporates were not creating a stimulating environment, or even asking their people to do that. They were not nurturing a caring, loving attitude towards people that really made a difference. I really wanted to change the world of work, the working environment and do something different and use my Human Resource skills to really get that ball rolling.

Seventeen

Logans

"Business opportunities are like buses, there's always another one coming." – Richard Branson

LOGANS WAS STARTED BY two young men in their late 20s, Russell, and Colin. I think both had come out of the auditing world although I'm not entirely sure about Colin. They were at school together at St Stithians College, and I think they both went to Wits. They got to know each other along the way, I'm not exactly sure how, probably through school connections and with both coming from very privileged families. Russell's father was certainly an entrepreneur in the mining industry, from a big granite mining family, and was very wealthy, and Colin from not as wealthy a background.

My connection to this partnership was through Russell, whom I met when I signed up to join the very yuppie Sandton Health and Racket Club, or The Sandton Wealth and Rolex Club as it was known then. This was where all the aspiring yuppies, merchant bankers, business owners, and wannabes went to do the body beautiful thing and get fit; some of us were there to meet girls, socialise and network and all sorts of things as well as get fit. Anyway, I met Russell there and he and I became training buddies which really meant helping each other out in the weights pit where we were doing free weight training. We used to "spot" each other - when you are picking up heavy weights, sometimes you need someone to do what's called "spot you" and just stand behind you or stand over you when you are doing a heavy lift, just in case your muscles fail on you. It was essential to have somebody else there to make sure that you were able to put the weight back on the weight stand or help you, so you didn't drop the weight and have it crush you.

Russell and I met that way, we were both similar shaped guys, 6 foot plus and I do admit we were both very vain at the time and we really cared what we looked like, we thought it was important. We loved womanising and perving and chatting up women, flirting and all sorts of things. We enjoyed partying together and we both had established groups of friends, mine from mainly university days at Rhodes, and his mainly from Wits. He was quite intimately involved in his Jo'burg school crowd and obviously the social crowd that he had established here. When we met up, it was quite interesting because I exposed him in a small way to my crowd, and funnily enough he wasn't immediately liked by my friends. They did get to know him and of course over time we all got on very well. Likewise he introduced me into his social circle of friends and that was quite an experience for me as I met quite a diverse group of people. At the time I had kind of had enough of the Rhodes sort of socialising pattern which usually revolved around heavy drinking and partying, and sometimes some sport whereas his circle of friends were into a little bit more of the sophisticated scene, the yuppie, restauranting, dating interesting girls, night clubbing, getting out on the town in the Johannesburg social setting. For me that was far more interesting, being something new and fresh, and also quite attractive from a social side.

Russell and I used to go to the gym in the evenings after work, and really get our day's frustration out on the metal, and ending with a shower and a steam bath. We would spend many hours doing the whole process of gyming and steam bathing, maybe followed by a bite or a meal somewhere. We spent ages chatting about life and about business and really what we were aspiring to do. Russell had done some articles with one of the big firms, but he had given it up and not finished his CA to go into an entrepreneurial venture with a friend of his, Colin. I recall they had both been lovers of skiing, and their privileged family upbringing had allowed them to go skiing once a year in the European ski season for probably the past four or five years. They were quite hooked on skiing as a hobby and a sport. Of course, in South Africa there's no snow so you have to head up north, particularly to Europe, being slightly cheaper than having to cross the pond and go all the way to the States. There were many, many wealthy South Africans that would make the pilgrimage with their family and friends for the skiing season, from about January to February or even sometimes earlier in December when the snowfall season in Europe begins. Consequently, they turned their hobby into a business and they started a small ski travel business. They then quickly convinced one of the big ski or travel wholesalers to take them on as a team to build a division of their company. This they did successfully and that was called Absolute Skiing. It was a very good part of this successful Beachcomber tour company, and they built this up very nicely. The owner of Beachcomber was a guy by the name of Terry and I think the three of them got on famously at the beginning, then they probably irritated the hell out of him by the success and speed at which they were able to build this business. There were obviously demands of bonuses and shares going on and eventually that didn't come to any fruit and Terry, Russell and Colin parted ways.

The two of them then started Logans with whatever the buyout agreement or the arrangement was for them exiting from the big tour company. They took some start-up capital that they had managed to put together and they started Logans as a tour operating wholesaler. They would create the packages and the travel agent network in South Africa would sell these to the consumer. Russell and Colin were exceptionally good at marketing these directly to the consumer, thereby creating the consumer demand. Clients would then go into the travel agents and say

"I want to book a Logans package, I've seen it on TV, I've heard it on the radio, I've seen it in the newspapers," etc. The prices were phenomenal as they had really good negotiating skills, and they were able to get really low priced, good value travel packages. Naturally the very sexy marketing behind it really drove consumer behaviour towards adoption and purchase of their packages instead of anybody else's. It was a very exciting business that they built, going from zero to about 200 million turn-over in less than two years. It was amazing and went from two people in a rented house, too close to one hundred and twenty young talented people rocking and rolling and creating all this value.

So I joined this entrepreneurial juggernaut. Russell floated an idea to me and said, "Man there's this thing called incentive travel, come and join us and let's sell some more travel together. It sounds interesting, and it should be up your street, it's related to motivating people, and you're in the people game, what about it?" So I said, "Russ, you know this is a great opportunity, I'd love to check it out!" In those days it was all about information, I read some brochures, I did some research and eventually I said "Russ, let me get on a plane and see what this is all about", so I got on a plane and I saw some companies in the UK and Asia and the US that were already in this space. I came back from researching a company that is still in existence today, and that I am still a great admirer of, and that was Maritz. Maritz Inc in the USA is a billion dollar incentive company that was really one of the founders of the incentive industry where jewellers in those days found a new way of selling their jewellery and their watches as long service awards. They built up the tradition of a long service award gold watch, and the golden handshake and all that kind of concept. Next they put together a catalogue of different long service awards and then developed their business into what it is today. Having seen the scope and this kind of scale, and the heights they had taken this business to so impressed me. I wanted to come back home to Africa and build a business that could one day be spoken of in similar terms to Maritz. Twenty years later a part of that dream has been fulfilled and I am very proud of that.

I came back from this trip rather inspired. I had not travelled extensively internationally, so joining a company that could put me on a career path, or rather an entrepreneurial path that also involved travelling the world, was a hugely exciting idea for me. Become a global yuppie? Wow! Break out of the Jo'burg yuppie scene and become a global yuppie, that was right up my alley! So I used my severance package from Barlows that would enable me to have several more months' safety net, and that's really what the start of my capital or the start of my journey was. I bought myself a PC, and my company car at the time was a 318 BMW, the little box shaped one that I absolutely loved. It was white, it was cool and it fitted my profile at the time, and I was away. I felt this huge sense of relief, of freedom at leaving the corporate world and being able to make my way and my own decisions and not worry about what the managing director or anyone else had to say. There was no more making decisions by committee, lobbying people for support and so on, it was just me and I felt free and light and fun and the smile came back on my face, but I never worked so hard in my whole life. I worked round the clock and fell asleep sometimes, but it was fascinating, and the energy and the passion and the excitement was just something that I was so grateful for. I still am grateful for that energy and the entrepreneurial freedoms. I love starting up businesses, I am a starter not an entrepreneur; I love starting things that can add value to peoples' lives and my own.

Well that was the start, and I moved in and made a little base in the small house that was being rented as the Logans offices, at the bottom of Rivonia, down Wessels road. I had a desk quite close to the kitchen. There were new people being employed all the time, and of course these new people were the best-looking girls that Russell and Colin could find. They were intelligent but there was a preference in the interviewing process for good looking people. On the whole it was a good-looking crowd of entrepreneurs and starters, and there were many distractions during the day, but people were focused and working hard. It really was a joy. It always has been a joy to be honest, and there have been very sad moments and challenging moments, but overall the journey has always been a great joy. I was meeting new people, making new friends and learning new things every day that I had not even contemplated in my corporate job. I was amazed at how much was going on and how much was required of me. I needed to be multi-skilled and multi-disciplined and thinking about hundreds of things rather than one singular professional pursuit.

That has always been the thing that has kept me engaged, fresh, and totally inspired - every day is a new learning, every client is a new opportunity to find out about how other people are running businesses, what other people are doing, in what industry sectors. It is truly inspirational being involved in multiple industry sectors rather than in the one business for life type of thing, because the big part of Uwin Iwin is a consultative business where we consult to multiple businesses in all sorts of industry sectors.

But I really came into this entrepreneurial juggernaut of Logans to start a division; I hadn't actually owned anything yet. I wasn't an owner, I wasn't a true entrepreneur, I was an employee but in another kind of context so that worried me. Early discussions started about "Hey, I actually want to run this division on my own, have an equity stake in it...", and the simple deal we did was make a three-way partnership. I said, "Russell you take a third, Colin you take a third, I'll take a third and we'll start a company." They agreed to that and then it was a process of registering this company and deciding on a name. But that's another story entirely.

Eighteen

The Sandman and the Hairy Carrot Company – or What's in a Name?

Proverbs 22:1 – "A good name is to be chosen rather than great riches, loving favour rather than silver and gold."

AT THE TIME WE were operating incentive travel programs for several clients. I remember some of my first clients being in the motor industry, Mercedes Benz was a big one but my actual first client was a spark plug company, NGK Spark Plugs. We were doing all sorts of travel trips for their dealer and distribution channels, and one of the things that we used to do well back then was, when we launched a programme, we would give it a theme and a great name. We still do all these things, but the other thing that I used to do at their sales conference was launch it with some kind of a video. Video Studio, the place where I got all my videos produced, also used to have a tremendously talented songwriter. I would tell this guy about the purpose of the programme, the ethos, the vibe that we wanted to communicate, and he would put together a song for the company and for the sales incentive, a real motivational, aspirational kind of song. Next the video guy would then put all the images together so it would be almost like a little mini music video production. That was quite a cool process in my business, and I loved going to the studio and getting it done and mixing with all the musos and all the creative types. It really got my creative juices going and we would sit for hours writing down the script of how this thing would play or pan out.

Forming this little company, we obviously went through all the registration processes and they ask you "What name are you going to give your company?" We had to give three options, so this guy Alan, who was also a previous marketer and an ad agency kind of guy, said "I'll give you a hand and let's think strategically and let's, you know… So tell me what this company is all about?" We pontificated and thought it through, and talked it round and round and eventually he said "Your company, you know it's about creating winners, and winners of these incentive trips and winners has got to go in somewhere, the name winners, winning, win, tell me a little bit more…" Then I came up with this concept of: we help you and the business win, and we do it by helping or empowering individuals within the business to also win, so a sort of win-win situation follows… Then Alan came up with the concept of "You win, I win", but not spelled YOU but rather the capital letter U – Uwin Iwin. As a name it somehow resonated with me and I thought this is pretty cool, in fact I loved it, so we went with Uwin Iwin, and winning something or other, and then tried to come up with a completely out-of-the-box name. We talked about the stick and the carrot, and we were the carrot providers, etc. At the time, ad agencies had this fashionable trend of naming themselves these crazy names like The Jupiter Drawing Room and The Shanghai Fire Cracker Factory, and I thought those were pretty cool. I kind of got into the trend of trying to think of an off the wall name so we came up with a third alternative for our company which was "The Hairy Carrot Company". Anyway, that wouldn't have worked now that I am bald… the Bald Carrot Company…

So we sent these three names off to the company registrar and they approved the first name which was Uwin Iwin Incentives and I proudly started my company with my third of the equity. My other two friends and business buddies also had an equal third. We started the business then created a logo, which was also inspired by the yuppiedom era: gold, greens, reds and a very complicated logo. Anyway, it served us well, we have evolved it since and simplified it and done some good things with our brand, but the name has always remained.

Nineteen

The Vibe

"Energy, like the Biblical grain of mustard seed, will move mountains." - Hosea Ballou

THE ENTREPRENEURIAL VIBE AT the time of starting a business is something very special. When people come together with a vision and are absolutely driven by passion and excitement, there's no better buzz. The energy of young people banding together as well, creating work, creating jobs, wanting to enter into an established economy, breaking in to be disruptive, bringing in that fresh thinking, that creative mindset, is an astounding generator of economic value. As much as the political agendas of the world are to maintain the status quo, one of the greatest mechanisms for changing the status quo is through entrepreneurialism. Bringing revolutionary ideas into a staid world through business is an amazing form of revolution. It's a revolution that brings forth passion and creativity and can substantially change things for the individuals involved, for all the stakeholders and for the world. We have seen how entrepreneurial ventures, especially in the tech space, have radicalised the way we think, the way we work and the way we live. The ones that take hold and gain traction are always for the advancement and the betterment of the world and the people in it.

My passion today is still much the same as it was back then. I reconnect with that energy daily; I try to encourage my teams and my start-ups to feel that same vibe, to generate that same buzz and to be part of a force for good, where they are creating their own destinies. They are shaping the environments and the economies that they are in, especially in Africa. It's phenomenal to see how the young people that I employ today are alive to the possibilities of making a major difference in their space and it is extremely exciting.

Going back to the original Logans days, I must say it was also not just all about work and serious behaviour. There was some crazy fun and hooligan behaviour and some things that I did back then that I am not proud of, but at the time it all seemed part of the whole vibe as we employed a huge amount of young people. My business was of course a smaller contribution to the bigger Logans group, and it was a very exciting time. Colin and Russell's early success really spurred them on to take on confidences that I have never seen before or after. Russell was such a confident artist, and he still is today. We have remained friends and he inspired many people around the world in his evangelism role for Herbalife, now on a global stage. He inspires young people to get involved in working for themselves, obviously now within the Herbalife framework, but Russell's confidence was always something that I completely admired. I suppose I took some of that confidence and I learned to grow it in myself and he helped encourage it in me.

Russell had this dream of also becoming the Richard Branson of Africa, and so he and Colin went off and negotiated with the bank to lease aircraft that they then flew from one of the American Boneyards across the Atlantic. Somehow these three planes arrived, and they launched an airline called Phoenix Air. I thought the name maybe had some bad vibes about it but the Phoenix was rising from the ashes, rising and making it. It was a tremendous success, huge in fact, and was one of the first low cost carriers in South Africa. It was immediately embraced by the public.

I was on the inaugural flight from Johannesburg to Cape Town. I made the pilot fly over the Cape Peninsula and do a bit of a round trip before landing. The power of being able to do that with a passenger airline, to be able to stand up in front of all the press and journalists and the first flush of passengers, and just ask the pilot to take the beautiful aircraft, which I think was a Boeing, and fly it around before landing was a rush, it was an absolute rush of note! Colin and Russell were on other legs, I think the Durban – Jo'burg leg and they were shuttling journalists up and down the whole day. But I got the Cape Town flight, I don't know why I was the lucky one who got it, but it is still a truly wonderful memory. It was a beautiful day in Cape Town, we were able to fly quite low over Cape Town itself and the harbour; and I remember going around Clifton and Sea point and thinking one day I'd have my mansion there on the beach. We then headed over Hout Bay, down to Cape Point, coming around again past Simon's Town, Muizenberg, and over the Strand area before eventually landing at Cape Town International Airport. It was an incredible vibe.

Other than that, I was not very much involved in that airline. Russell's brother came in to operationalise the staffing and management of that. Colin was really focussed on Logans, Russell was running around borrowing money from banks, sourcing funding and all sorts of things, and it was a success then. Unfortunately, the impact that launching an airline had on the cashflow started to take its toll.

The parties were epic. Logans was the first wholesaler to do an annual travel agent bash and I think the first bash was 400+ travel agents at Gallagher Estate. It was a massive party, with a private DJ, smoking and festivities. Being the young guns that they were, Colin and Russell really were loved by the young people that were in the travel agency channel, and they vibed and really connected at a different level to all the other competitors at the time.

Our staff Christmas party I remember because Logans had it on a party boat at Hartbeespoort Dam which was also epic. How we didn't lose somebody to drowning that night with the amount of tequila and other beverages that were consumed, heaven alone knows. But the partying and the good times were a wonderful way of releasing the stress that came with working exceptionally long hours and being really focussed. It was good, and my little organisation was also growing. We had our own part of the office complex now. We had moved from the house into a place called Eden Park which was a very upmarket A-grade office space, and I had probably a hundred square metres of that for my team of around ten people at Uwin Iwin. We had running account managers, we had creative people, we were doing video production and campaign management as well as the travel fulfillment, and it was all going quite well. I was travelling the world and exploring new destinations for our potential customers, it was extremely exciting, and I was really riding a high. Success bred confidence and there was plenty on the go, but unfortunately there were signs of stress in the organisation, and I'll elaborate further on.

Here I have to mention my father who was bitterly disappointed that I had decided to end my corporate career, because he saw his son on a pretty good trajectory with blue chip organisations. I suppose in his old school way he had envisaged a long career for me, hopefully ending up pretty high or at the top of some organisation. He didn't think of his son as an entrepreneur. He obviously knew the entrepreneurial hardships having done the entrepreneurial thing with his dad, gone on to corporate and then back to the entrepreneurial world. Nonetheless he was tremendously proud of me as he always was, and I've always had his 100% support, but I was at a time of my life when my parents weren't really a big part of the equation. I was independent, I was making money, I was being successful, family wasn't that important to me, and I was just having fun and doing my own thing.

Twenty

First Employee

"Individual commitment to a group effort - that is what makes a team work, a company work, a society work, a civilisation work." - Vince Lombardi

STARTING UWIN IWIN AMONGST this entrepreneurial energy of course required me to hire my first employee. I had hired many people before in my career in human resources, but that was always hiring people for somebody else to manage and nurture; I had not employed many people to work for me. I needed to find a very skilled travel person as many of our first incentives were travel programmes that needed to be planned, costed, managed and executed. I needed that person to be able to travel to international destinations with incentive group winners, give them the "white glove, red carpet" treatment and manage every single aspect of the event, then bring the guests back safely, having had a fantastic time.

I put out an advert and interviewed a number of candidates, but one really caught my attention. Her energy was good, she was a lovely looking young lady, and I think she had just turned 21. This was Gail. She was a tall redhead and there was something about her that I really liked. I was right, she was a gem of a hire, and we worked together for very many years; she eventually became a director and shareholder in the business and a very good friend as well. Gail had an amazing work ethic, she was an attention to detail fanatic and she had an incredible customer service value. But the interview was quite funny. She got the call to come to a late afternoon interview with myself, in the middle of a picnic that she and her sisters were on, and there was quite a bit of alcohol involved in the picnic lunch or whatever it was. So, she arrived with a few tequilas and glasses of wine under her belt, a fact she only disclosed to me in later weeks, after she was employed. She said she couldn't believe she got the job, when she wasn't altogether sober! I remember this very energetic, enthusiastic, bubbly, smiley faced 21-year-old walking into my office. I was about 28 or 29 at the time, so we related well in the generational sense.

We started working as a team, and Gail and I really learnt the incentive travel business together because her background was in retail travel, she had done a diploma in that, and of course incentive travel was a whole new kettle of fish. But we really did well, we put our heads down, we worked hard, and we put together some phenomenal programmes. She was the travel professional and I was the sales jockey, and together we made a very good combination. As the business grew we hired other people, but I think it was Gail's real hardworking, ethical and determined customer focus that really set the tone for what was to come in terms of an operational strength that we had. Our clients felt it, and we felt it. We felt confident about what we were doing, we were passionate about the business, we delivered in detail, we understood the costing models and it was really a powerful combination.

· · · • · • · • · · ·

Throughout my career I have always hired and preferred to hire for attitude and passion, rather than necessarily what was on your CV in terms of academics. Gradually our businesses evolved to become a little bit more academic, but I always seek that spark in a person that really tells me that not only does the CV look good, but the personality and the values fit too. This is such a key aspect to me when I hire people, because when I've got that wrong, it has cost me dearly. Now that I am not doing all the hiring, I have had to train others to look for similar kinds of fit for our business. It's imperative to find the right people for your business and I pay plenty of lip service to the fact that people are a business's strongest asset. This certainly is the case in a service business, you do not rely necessarily on the quality of your brand or your product, you are reliant on a day to day basis on the ability of your team of people to connect with your customers, to deliver on your promises and to be very good problem solvers along the way because incidents happen, things do go wrong, and it's how you deal with those moments that determines the long-term sustainable value in the service business. We've had so many examples of how tough, challenging and sometimes ugly situations have been our opportunity to shine with our values, to be honest, to think outside the box, and think creatively in order to solve a business challenge. That is a testimony to and a quality that any business should have: people that are prepared to go that extra mile, work late nights, work together as a team to solve problems, engage in a partnership relationship with a customer, rather than a transactional relationship where we put the best interests of our customers first and ours are secondary. Our focus is really on how we can deliver, because delivery is everything. You are only as good as your last service delivery.

For a service business that has been in operation for 21 years, there's no end time, there's no half time, and you're always on. You must achieve a balance between that relentless pursuit of customer service and making sure that the people that are servicing those needs are well looked after. They must take breaks and holidays when they need to. As a business owner you must equip the people in your business with the right skills and resources to do their job efficiently, and that is a constant challenge. I always say to my team, "My job as the CEO is to make sure you have the right resources in order to do an excellent job. Your job is to take those tools and resources and apply them in a way that keeps our customers happy and meets the business objectives."

This is the message that we preach to customers: if you want to accelerate your business, grow your revenues, and become what you are focussed on, then you have to take care of the people in your business and in your channels, and inspire them to always deliver at their highest level. I say to my team constantly, "If a customer walks through our doors and doesn't get the feeling that they're in a business where people are inspired to be their best, then how can we preach that message if we are not living it?" Of course, there are times when we have failed our employees and I am not proud of those moments, but those are few and far between. We are striving to make sure those moments are fewer and further between, we want to really stimulate those in our business environment. At least I can honestly say that from the get-go I was able to develop that within our business.

Twenty-One

Marketing Creativity and Culture

"Culture is simply a shared way of doing something with a passion." – Brian Chesky

IN THE EARLY DAYS, one of the things that I really learnt from that entrepreneurial mega ride was the consistent theme of the creative and marketing culture. Logans was a company that really resonated in the marketplace. We were all about our strong culture, and the culture was a young, dynamic, vibrant, disruptive start-up. Probably 90% of all travel agents in that sector, that would use a wholesaler like Logans in the early days, happened to be young people, between the ages of nineteen, twenty to about thirty. They were looking for something different as the travel industry was a bit staid, and rather boring in fact, for an industry that should have been be funky and vibey, offering opportunities to see the world and make the world your oyster. Logans certainly created this aura, this culture of young, dynamic and funky. They had sexy brochures, and incredible travel opportunities. The marketing was tied in with a TV program called "Wish you were here" which was an early travelogue type program that gained huge traction. It was a massive success and of course the parties were legendary. There was an annual travel agents get-together where awards were given out and there was always a huge turnout. This also contributed to the momentum and that culture rocked the travel world. All the staid, existing travel wholesalers were just blown away by the power of the juggernaut that was this new culture.

You couldn't really call it a strategy. Peter Drucker talks about how culture beats strategy hands down, and I believe it. I saw it in action and it's something I have always carried with me as a business leader, nurturing the culture and the Uwin Iwin culture. At the core of the business are transparency, honesty and integrity, and we build out from there, using creativity, energy, winning formulas and customer centricity. What our culture is all about is being professional and making sure that we do what we say we're going to do, whilst really nurturing our team and having fun. We nurture our customers too and help them win. The marketing element is essential, and so is keeping it fun, fresh and relevant. For many years I kind of lost track of how important marketing was. Of course as an entrepreneurial business you don't have big marketing budgets and hence you tend to stay away from it because you just can't afford it, but in today's digital revolution, every business can afford to market quite aggressively on the internet and through social media for relatively small costs. You don't have to take double page spreads in the Sunday Times to catch peoples' attention, you don't have to have TV and radio budgets; you can really operate within the online space. A couple of years ago I set the task of being Best in Class in terms of digital marketing, and since then we have invested so much in that space and the returns are always fresh. You can amplify your culture, you can touch people deeply with it, and you can win the hearts and minds through good dynamic advertising and digital marketing.

Creativity for me is an absolute no-brainer. One has to look at how one can do things differently, create a message and a service that adds massive amounts of value, and is what the customer wants. It must be delivered in fresh, exciting ways, and that's really the heart of, or the seeding ground of where innovation comes from. It doesn't come from sitting down and saying "Ah well, now we have to be innovative", it has to be inbred into the DNA of who you are, and how you offer things to customers. If you start by applying creativity to the way in which you're going to keep it fresh and relevant for people, out of that grows a desire to do things differently, to add value, to innovate, to always remain up to date in terms of looking around and using what's new and funky and fresh out there, to enhance what you have. We've done that many times, just re-thinking something that is fresh and innovative and then delivering on the ground for that. Most entrepreneurial start-ups and new businesses today have identified how important that is along with the dynamic people that drive all of that, so culture for me is fundamental. From a good culture you can build your wildest dreams, and reach them, especially if you have people that buy into those dreams of course. Now that is another ballgame in itself!

Twenty-Two

Belief

"Self-confidence is contagious."- Stephen Richards

IN ORDER TO REALLY achieve I had to focus on a belief. The belief for me came from sitting in a corporate environment, observing some suppliers that interacted with our business and thinking "Wow, that's doable, I could do the same. I could go out there and do it; I'm probably a little bit smarter than they are!" I had that belief; I had the energy and I had the passion. But the belief must come from a level of self-confidence, a confidence that's deep within one's soul, and it's a fundamental that takes you through some of the darkest hours of the entrepreneurial journey. At the beginning of the process I certainly believed, and what exactly did I believe in? Well, in truth, the number one starting position was I believed in myself, and I believed that if I had set my heart and mind to something, I could do it. Thinking back on that, that self-belief was nurtured by my father. He always said that I could do it, I could achieve, I could overcome, and that his confidence in me was great. My own self-confidence then grew from taking a leaf out of that book. I learnt to believe, then achieve, slowly at first with small steps of achievement. I certainly never was the rocket scientist in the class, in fact I was very average academically, and I was never the sporting hero, but there were a couple of things that I did excel in. I was and am reasonably sporty, but I think the nurturing thought is that if you try to do something, and you believe you can do it well, you can achieve it. The other thing that stays in my mind is that you don't have to outrun the competition by a million miles - you just have to be 1% better than them. You just have to be one step ahead when the finish line comes on winning a deal. You don't have to be a hundred steps ahead, you just have to be a little bit ahead, and beating mediocrity is a huge part of success. I'm blessed that I am not necessarily a perfectionist, so for me I don't have to be perfect before I go to market. I must have enough confidence that what I have in the bag is one percent better than the competition. This has always served me well, because I've been able to hit the market with an agile, lean, quick solution that has a quality thread in it. I can then sell the concept and I continually bring my team alongside to innovate, shape and build a greater level of quality and depth and fill out the other legs of the opportunity or solution. But there's that overriding belief that stems from the knowledge that I can do it and my team can do it with me. This is absolutely crucial to the process and I always had that in myself from day one. I believed in myself. The environment that I was in and the other guys that I worked with had self-confidence that oozed all over the page. They were both exceptionally confident, especially Russell. Russell came from an extremely wealthy family where I think the whole notion of "I will be a gladiator, I will be the top performer, I will be the emperor", was just ingrained in their whole psyche. Russell certainly helped me to lift my head and set my goals higher than I was probably able to do on my own. However it was that infectiousness of confidence and the feeling that we could do anything, including smashing through some of the stereotyped mindsets of what a young guy can do, that was a blast, an absolute blast.

The second thing about belief is how do you believe in what you do? Do you believe in what you are doing – is it fundamentally good, will it produce a result that is fundamentally better for the world? Can you shift the world, and the people that you interact with in your world? Will it make a difference, will it inspire, will it drive things forward, is this a part of progress and do you believe in it yourself? I'm a great believer in making people's environment more aspirational and inspiring. The more you provide the right, creative, fertile environment in which people can lift their game and perform, the more people will strive to achieve because they inherently want to better themselves. Betterment is part of human nature, culture and civilisation, people want to move forward. I don't believe for one minute that people do not want to get ahead. We believed in what we did, so we took that philosophy and looked at how we could drive that within the business environment. How could we make peoples' lives richer and better, how could we give people the opportunities to win and get ahead? We had to basically answer the question that so many people ask: "Well what's in it for me? If I work harder or go the extra mile, what's in it for me?" I really believed in what we were doing and I was able to crystalize that early on. Self-confidence and self-belief, belief in yourself as well as in what you are doing, make a powerful component for lifting and moving forward.

The other profound thing about belief for me is the belief and trust in God. Now this didn't come in the beginning, it only came after my huge fall. I know about spiritual belief, belief that God loves me, and if God loves me it means God wants to see me move forward in a way that is meaningful, that I can fulfil my dreams and visions, I can make a positive impact on people and the world around me. The combination of three things, belief and love of myself, combined with the love of what I do, and alongside the love of God, is what I believe to be a significant factor in the belief equation. The three components make up a considerable energy stream that can move one forward and change your destiny.

• • • • • • • • • • •

I wanted to make a difference and having this powerful belief that I could make a difference, I had to put a concept together, some marketing collateral and then of course hit the road and sell! Now selling wasn't a skill I thought I had in my briefcase, so I piled into a couple of really good books about selling. I started knocking on doors and hitting the phones and getting appointments, and to my disbelief I overcame this crazy notion that selling was difficult! I started to love it. Going out, meeting new people, talking to them and having conversations, listening to what they had to say, listening to their business needs, telling them my story and then trying to get a deal together after writing proposals and doing some costings, wow, it is so exciting! Today as group CEO, I'm still most juiced when I am in front of a customer selling. Nowadays the sale is a lot more technical and we need to have specialists in the room but it's still the same. It is conversation, it's presenting, it's putting your best foot forward and it's going for it.

· · ● · ● · ● · ● · · ·

My first client was NGK Spark Plugs and my second client was in the motor industry, Mercedes Benz. I went from not having any customers, to having a few customers that were paying the bills and making some inroads. It was tremendously exciting and it still is exciting today. From an entrepreneurial point of view, ideas are great, and they must have some sort of room for growth until you get traction and adoption of your ideas and concepts by your client. This is usually done in a sales environment, and of course with today's online apps, it can also be done in the digital space. Selling is a wonderful asset to have in your arsenal, and I believe that every single person can sell. We're presenting ourselves; we're pitching ideas and we're having conversations to convince somebody that our idea is a good idea and can add value. I have always encouraged every single member of my team to think of themselves as a salesperson. In any environment, be it in an elevator, or at home, or around a fire, in a living room, they must be able to articulate what we do and why we do it and be able to tell the story. It doesn't matter who you are in the business, you should be able to do that anywhere and either channel that opportunity, if there is one, to the sales team or to someone that can then go and score the goal. So, in the early days I found myself kind of going from zero to hero in a rather quick time frame and it was fantastic. It was really encouraging, and it built so much self confidence in what we were doing. When the market accepts you and your brand, your idea and your concept and wants to work with you, there's no better feeling or confidence boost. On the other hand, however, you need to have a thick enough skin to be able to take the rejections, and that's always the balance and the very humbling factor. In sales, you can't win them all but you certainly need to win enough to keep ahead of the game, keep the wolf from the door and keep the engines rolling. The sales game is one that needs to be embraced in a far bigger and more meaningful way in business today. Many business schools teach about all sorts of things other than sales, yet if your organisation can't sell, no matter who you are and what kind of industry you are in, you're going to be left in the lurch.

Twenty-Three
Zero to Hero

"Failure is success if we learn from it." – Malcolm Forbes

GOING FROM ZERO TO hero also brings a new set of complexities with it. The ability to handle the service aspect of your business as you're growing, that's the one dynamic. The other dynamic is to keep your ego in check because you can get really carried away when things are going well. You can completely stir up your emotional well-being by the fact that you're on a winning streak, but the moment the troubled times come, you've also got to be able to cope with that and have a contingency plan in place. I was very fortunate always to have incredibly good operational people in the team that were able to deliver at a high customer service level, and very early in the game I was roped in by my operations people to be told "Do not promise these ridiculous things that we can't deliver on!" Again, that was a balanced game between being able to be innovative and therefore customer centric, and able to customise your offering to a particular customer, and in so doing, creating an operational problem for yourself on being able to deliver this unique masterpiece every time you go out and sell. In the service domain, where my business predominately is, we are not selling widgets or vehicles or things, we are selling concepts and ideas. These concepts and ideas can be executed in a way that is sustainable and actually delivers results. It's a tremendously interesting concept of selling because really, every time you are sitting in front of a unique customer, in a different industry sector, the ability to think on your feet, where you are able to translate concept theory and knowledge into a particular solution for a customer, is a much needed skill. Obviously, you always have to, in the back of your head, be able to ask yourself "Can I actually deliver on this unique offering?" I must admit there were times where we had to wing it, and at those times I wasn't 100% happy with the delivery, but I always challenged the operational teams to stay nimble and dynamic and able to meet the customer requirements. Doing this I also discovered a side of me that became really creative in the selling process, and I think the early adopters of our services loved the freshness, the young thinking, the forward-thinking approach that we tried to inject into our proposals. We did some fun, crazy things, and I remember once selling, to Pfizer Pharmaceuticals, an incentive travel trip to Mexico. When we arrived in the lobby, myself and two other members of our team, dressed with huge Mexican hats, sambas and some music going that was really, truly authentic Mexican fiesta, people looked at us like we were crazy. We walked into the boardroom where serious executives from that big pharmaceutical company were seated, and they looked at us and they thought we were insane. We then took the whole idea of this destination and the excitement, and we brought it alive in a boardroom setting. It really won the hearts and the minds of these execs who, at the end of the meeting, couldn't wait to get themselves and their teams to qualify for the incentive destination that we had proposed. Naturally we won the business, but it was a little bit risky and out-the-box. Sometimes that works, other times it doesn't, but it's a case of knowing when to push that innovation button. In business, sometimes we get too damn serious about who we are and try to complicate things; we complicate our proposals with fancy academic terminology so that we can keep up with the benchmark consulting firms in the world, and really that gets tired and boring sometimes. People have heard it all and they don't want to necessarily buy another business school case study experience, they are looking for something genuine and unique. Being real and authentic, being yourself and bringing that true DNA into the picture is sometimes incredibly valuable to do.

Coming back to keeping the ego in check, well I learnt that lesson the hard way when the fall came. Ego and materialism and living the yuppie dream is one thing, but building a business is a long term game. Sure, have fun, celebrate your successes and that kind of thing, but never, ever get ahead of yourself and feel that invincibility. Confidence has to be checked with humility and even as confident as I am today, I always approach a new pitch with some kind of level of butterflies in the tummy. The trick is to get them to fly in formation in the moment, but also to be really reliant and humble enough to say a little prayer beforehand and say a prayer of gratitude afterwards if you're able to perform and give a good presentation. That keeps me level headed and sane, and I always believe that cockiness and overconfidence is something that not everybody warms to. Humility and sincerity are a much better formula for any approach. You have to demonstrate your confidence, but not in a way that is brash and garish in the approach.

Twenty-Four

Uwin Iwin, Geneva & Cultural Experiences

"I would rather own little and see the world than own the world and see little of it." - Alexander Sattler

As I MENTIONED BEFORE, I was part of a young travel business that was really booming, but I didn't leave my corporate job to become an employee of another company. I had told Colin and Russell that I needed to start my own business within the business, forming a three-way partnership. In hindsight, that wasn't a very clever thing to do, but they had the infrastructure, the accounting infrastructure, they were the ones that had given me the opportunity and I was very happy with that. We had settled on the name of Uwin Iwin, creating winning solutions for the business as our corporate customer, and by empowering and creating winning opportunities for the individuals in those businesses. Really one of the big mistakes that I made early in the business was paying so much attention to the marketing, sales and customer service side of the business that I wasn't really paying too much attention to the financial side. I thought I had it covered in that we had an accounts department that was running and overseeing the business. We were doing the invoicing; they were doing the banking and reconciliation and so on. But I really wasn't in control of what was happening financially in my business and that is a huge mistake to any entrepreneur. From the very beginning you have to know where every cent and rand or dollar in your business is going, what you're spending it on , or how you plan to spend it. You need to keep track of your budgets, your performance against budgets and targets, the variances, the whys, the wherefores, and really know all of the components of the business.

But having said that, Uwin Iwin was a business I was very fortunate to get into and I absolutely loved it. It was a business where I was using my skills to consult to other businesses about how they could increase the performance of their people, and at that stage we were singularly offering travel incentives as the outcome. With the travel incentive aspect, I was very fortunate to get into the big wide world of travel. I started getting invited to trade shows and familiarisation or fam-trips as they were known. I got invited to see destinations, to visit places like Singapore and Australia and all sorts of exotic destinations, and these were fully paid for, usually involving a business class upgrade from the airline, and fancy 5-star hotels on the other side. All meals and tours and other things were taken care of too, and of course that was a great perk to the business. I never had the opportunity, or never wanted the opportunity to have an overseas post-school or post-university experience like some of my buddies had done, but this was the way to see the world for me, and gee whizz, I think it was just like a dream come true. Flying here and flying there, being part of a global industry and getting to meet other entrepreneurs, other professionals in the business, it was a tremendous thing. I was 29 years old; I was flying high literally and seeing the world in totally unique ways. It was an incredible rush.

· · · · ● · ● · · ·

The early days of being an entrepreneur with my own business were tremendously exciting and fast paced as I've said many times before. This global ability to move around the planet, visit different places, do business and see things, and propose new destinations to clients was a very big part of my personal growth experience. It set new horizons for me, further horizons than I had ever dreamed of. But this young entrepreneurial environment wasn't always that healthy. Yes, we were working incredibly long hours which took its toll on the body; I was gyming furiously with Russell Monday to Thursday, and completely overdosing on partying, boozing, eating, drinking and dancing and all the good things, or sometimes the not so good things. I had a consciousness about my lifestyle and myself becoming unhealthy, and that I wasn't necessarily coping with the same pace as some of the other guys were seemingly able to cope with, especially when it came to drinking and quantities of alcohol intake. I remember sitting down for lunch with Russell once, at a place called Manhattans, and was introduced to a new drink called a Margarita, a tequila and lemon-based drink that we ordered by the jug. The first jug was consumed, and the second jug was ordered, and I got up from the table and I nearly couldn't make it to the gents. I couldn't walk in a straight line and I just knew that the alcohol consumption was not sitting well with me, and I wasn't coping, but even with that consciousness, I wasn't yet prepared to do anything about it, because it was fun.

• • • •●•● • • •

Every year there was a massive trade show held in Geneva, and the first time I went to this was in my first year of operation. It was mind-blowing, the size and the scale of this exhibition. You basically arrived in Geneva on a Swissair flight, got shuttled to a hotel, then you arrived at this massive conference or exhibition centre, and the world had showed up in one place! Every exhibition stand represented a different country. You were able to go from Sweden to Denmark, to Russia, to India, to China and all in the space of a couple of hundred metres. You met people speaking different languages everywhere you turned. The reason for being there was to build up partnerships and networks. It was an opportunity for guys in these foreign destinations to sell you their services, so that when you were planning tours for your incentive clients, you'd consider them and you'd know a local partner that could help deliver the quality experience you were looking for.

I was informed that the party to be at that night was the Las Vegas party. The Las Vegas team had a budget second to none, to lavish on creating the Vegas experience wherever they go in the world. So the Las Vegas tourism board and all the Vegas destination management companies got together and they rented out a particular bar in Geneva. It was all the drink you can possibly consume, and it was really an amazing party. Of course I loved this, relished the opportunity, and I met some very interesting guys, one of whom, Alan Waxler, I am still friends with today.

I think Alan is from Italian descent. He liked to think of himself as a big mover and shaker, and he was a big cigar smoking, macho Las Vegas host. Alan could get you in anywhere, get you tickets to any show, he knew everybody, and he still does. More than that, as a professional, he was also a great party animal, he knew all the girls and it was good fun to be around old Alan. These parties went on late into the night and they were intense. Later on I got to go to these Las Vegas parties when I was in Chicago at the Chicago trade show, and on an annual basis the Las Vegas party in Geneva became a really big hit before they moved the show to another destination.

I had the huge advantage of being connected globally to people as a South African, coming from a relatively sheltered and isolated economic background, and now having the world open up to me. It was a tremendously powerful experience. It motivated me in a way that still resonates today. I am connected to and in relationships with many people around the world. I have immense gratitude for those relationships that have created opportunities and business connections beyond my wildest expectations.

• • • ● • ● • • • •

One fun learning experience I can remember is being invited to visit Singapore by the Singapore Tourism Board. Flying business class on Singapore Airlines, we landed in Singapore early in the morning. I felt a little bit jet-lagged because it was one of the first trips I did to the East. I was culturally out of my depth, surrounded by predominantly Chinese speakers or Chinese, Singaporean, Malay and Asian cultures. Apart from having Chinese takeaway at home, I don't think I'd ever really dined in a formal, upmarket Chinese restaurant before. We landed, we got checked into our hotel very early, and then we were out on a bus to see a number of 5-star hotels. Coming from Johannesburg, I hadn't been in that many high-rise buildings in my life. Of course, Singapore is a city of many high rise buildings, high rise hotels and these superfast elevators. You get in and press the button, the door closes, and then it feels like you have left your stomach on the ground floor while your head soars up to the 15th and 20th floors by the time you have even blinked your eyes. The combination of the jetlag, these high rise elevator rides up and down, up and down, on multiple floors to go and see various different suites with different room categories in each of these hotels, you can imagine I wasn't feeling that great. To top it all, for our first meal, we were taken into this phenomenal hotel, it was the Orient Hotel or something like that, and the GM and all his minions were there. They brought out this massive, lavish spread of Chinese food and I'll never forget the first course were these tiny, tiny button mushrooms that were oily and slippery but quite delicious once you got hold of them. The only implement to feed yourself with were these beautiful, elaborately carved Chinese chopsticks, and it goes without saying that my Chinese chopsticks skills weren't great. I nonetheless pursued and chased these little button mushrooms around the plate because I was quite hungry, even though I was jet-lagged and a bit queasy from the elevator rides. We ploughed through 12 courses of Chinese formal cuisine and it was a delightful experience. Being hungry and being a great adventurous foodie, I was obviously demonstrating a joyful experience at this lunch table, and our hosts were so pleased that I loved the food and wanted to have more. I later found out that it's not good protocol to finish everything at a Chinese meal because they will keep bringing you food until you just cannot eat any more. It's good to leave food on the plate because that means you are satisfied and have had enough.

· · · ● · ● · ● · ·

So that was my baptism of fire of cross-cultural experiences in the world of travel, and the world of business and I'll be forever grateful for the incredible experiences my business journey has taken me on. So many different countries, I think in excess of 50 countries, that I have been able to experience at a truly high end level, with clients, with educational tours, with attending trade shows, with becoming members of professional associations. It was really, really cool and I suppose the one downside is that I couldn't really translate these global experiences that easily to my local friends, because every time I started telling them these wonderful stories, I'd get this look of disbelief as people thought I was exaggerating. Eventually people were tired of hearing my stories of exotic lands and far-away destinations and I started telling less and less stories about these wonderful experiences. They almost became singular in the experiential domain, it was my experiences locked up in my little cupboard, or my little bottle and in one way I am a bit saddened by that. But thankfully I then met a phenomenal woman who agreed to become my wife and we were able to share many of these experiences in the early days and travel together.

Twenty-Five

Meeting my Darling

"Love is our true destiny. We do not find the meaning of life by ourselves alone - we find it with one another." - Thomas Merton

As you can imagine in this environment of male hedonism where I was earning good money and I was entrepreneurially free, I had many girlfriends and opportunities for relationships, left, right and centre. It was really an environment or a lifestyle that was, for the first time in all my dating or relational history, where I had this freedom. I was freewheeling, I was on a roll and the guys that I was with were also on the same buzz. Nothing was serious, relationships were short term and it was just party, party, party.

Then in amongst that dropped this pearl, this jewel of an opportunity to have a relationship with a woman of great integrity, who also had a wonderful mind and was beautiful. This dream lady had sparkled onto the scene, and I was hugely conflicted. I knew that I had to make a lifestyle choice between the road that I was on, or a road less travelled, which was a road of commitment and long-term relationship and marriage. That scared the daylights out of me, but it was clear for me that I had a choice to make. I am so glad that I made the right choice and picked a long-term focused vision for my life in a relationship with a woman. Today I can say I am delighted that we have been married for quite some time, in excess of 20 years now. We still care for and love each other and have an ongoing vision of being together for the rest of our lives.

That moment when I met Dorcas, I had taken a breather from partying. I had bought a small house in Sunninghill, a beautiful little thatch duplex that was my first house. I paid a deposit and I was paying the bond, but I had kind of neglected the interior design of this place for a while. So, I decided "This is the weekend I am not drinking anymore. Instead of going to the pub straight after work on Friday afternoon and following the normal routine of a weekend, I am going to the hardware store to buy some paint!" I had a little vision for the bathroom, and I was going to sort the bathroom out, so that's what I did. I came home, put on some music, had some takeout I think then put on an old pair of shorts and a shirt and I started painting the bathroom. It was rather lonely, but I really got into it, painting and jiving to the music. I was on my own mission and I was actually quite happy not to be going out. But I finished up, and I looked at the job that I had done and I said "Wow, I've done a good job. I feel great that I have done this, but now what?"

I wondered where the lads were, and I started imagining the various places they might be. I thought perhaps I should go and see what was going on, and obviously my curiosity of what they were doing, and maybe what millennials today refer to as the fear of missing out, took hold. I had a shower, scrubbed some paint off me, made an attempt with my hair and got in my car. At about 10.30 that night I set off into Rosebank to a pub called Hoods. Hoods was a favourite stomping ground of ours; it was very trendy, mostly young people, many good-looking girls, so I found a parking spot and headed into Hoods.

As I walked in the door this beautiful tall blonde that I recognised was walking towards me, and on her way out she greeted me and said, "Oh, hello", and I said "Hi Dorcas, how are you, haven't seen you for ages..." and her friend Helen was there in tow as always. I asked Helen how she was doing also, and we all had a quick conversation and then they left, and

I went in. I didn't see my mates anywhere, and little did I know that Dorcas had said to Helen, "Helen, I'm going back in, I want to spend some more time with David" and long story short they came back in. We met up again, I bought them drinks and we had a nice chat. By that time, it was nearly midnight already and we decided to leave. I walked out to my little BMW parked there and I said "Cheers!" Dorcas said to me "Tomorrow we're going to a braai, with a whole lot of old Rhodes people" and I arrogantly turned around and said "Listen, I don't do braais anymore." I had left that Rhodes university crowd and the braaing and the partying around the pool scene, and I was trying to meet other kinds of friends, so the braaing and Rhodes parties weren't my kind of thing anymore. So I told her this and she took that as a real snub as I later came to find out.

But somehow that then sparked both her and my interest. A couple of days later I got a phone call from Helen, saying "We're going out to the Rattlesnake Roadside Diner", which was also a very trendy, cool spot in Rivonia, "Would you like to come along?" So I asked Helen who was asking me, was it herself or Dorcas? "No, no," she said, "Dorcas would like you to come", so I said that's fine, because that was the answer I was hoping for. Helen and I are still great friends today but I wasn't interested in Helen, I was interested in Dorcas. Dorcas had twisted Helen's arm to make the call and invite me, and of course I pitched up at this dinner at the Rattlesnake Roadside Diner because I wanted to know what was going on. We had a lovely evening except that then Dorcas decided to tell me my fortune in no uncertain terms, how she thought I was an arrogant, young asshole and that I needed to think about my life more clearly. I can't remember exactly what she said but I just remember thinking "Wow okay, if I had invited someone on a date I may have been a bit nicer, to get the second date!" After that I really thought it was all over and the end of the line on that one.

As things would have it, Dorcas had actually said to Helen, "This is the guy I am going to marry" and Helen was absolutely shocked and devastated because I suppose in that moment you couldn't have got two more different people. Dorcas and I are still two very, very different people. She was academically minded in university, she did her honours in English and Linguistics, and she was a very responsible young lady from a conservative home. She herself was conservative and religious from a practising Catholic family background. I would say she was a prim and proper lady, and I was anything but a gentleman. Of course I always had good manners, I was brought up well but I had this perception of maybe being a little bit of a bad boy, somewhat rebellious, alternative, certainly not a private school prat, but from a very different mould and mindset. So Helen was shocked because this was so out of character for Dorcas, and she wanted to know what the story was, and why Dorcas was so into this guy.

Anyway, we had a few more dates that went much better than the Rattlesnake Diner date. We had a tremendous time one evening at a place called Chentos in Bedfordview, where I tried to articulate this conflict that I had in my head between a hedonistic lifestyle and a committed relationship lifestyle. I tried to tell Dorcas that I was at this critical junction or crossroads and I was struggling with it. She thought I was trying to break up with her and I had to convince her I wasn't! There were tears on both sides of the table that night, but after that evening, having spoken it out, and having had to answer some quite difficult questions from Dorcas, I knew that this was the girl with whom I wanted to spend the rest of my life.

I wanted to take a path that was less travelled at the time, a path of commitment and long-term relationship. I realised this really was who I was as a person, it was in my DNA. This other lifestyle that I was living now was somebody else's lifestyle that I was living out and following, and although it was fun, it wasn't really me. I finally was being true to myself, and not long after that we decided to get engaged. I proposed to Dorcas, she says I didn't, but I did...

She says I didn't, I say I did!

We went to a beautiful Conservation Company lodge called Phinda in northern Natal. It was a spectacular place, incredible game drives and lodges and we were thoroughly spoilt, living this luxury lifestyle. After dinner we got into bed together, and I said to her "Will you marry me?" Perhaps I had said that in my head a hundred times, but maybe I didn't say it out loud, she says I didn't, I say I did! Eventually I said to her "And so, what's your answer" and she said "Well, what's the question?" So I said "Will you marry me?" and she said yes of course, and it was a wonderful moment. We then had to wait a little bit because I went away on a trip, and once I came back I had to ask permission from her mum and dad. It was a long drive down to Grahamstown in order to do that. We went and got a ring made and it was a tremendous time of our lives. We set the wedding date, yes it was quick, but we knew what we wanted. I certainly knew what I wanted, and she knew what she wanted, so it was a case of "Let's not mess around with this, let's get married, set a date and do it", which we did.

Twenty-Six
A Wedding to Remember

"...true love is never blind, but rather brings an added light." - Phoebe Cary

OUR ACTUAL WEDDING WAS also a tremendous story on its own. We got married in Grahamstown because Dorcas's mum and dad lived there and it was also where I went to university, so I was comfortable with that. We decided that we would get married in the Catholic Church because she was from a Catholic background, and it would please her mother. For me a church was a church so I didn't really care that much at that time. I was obviously from an Anglican family background and it didn't really worry me too much that it was a Catholic church. We had to go and talk to the Catholic priest, and we did what we needed to do to get it done. We set up this church service at the Catholic Church in Grahamstown, and we left most of the planning of the party to the people who were down in Grahamstown, which were Dorcas's mum and dad. We went and scouted out a few venues: the venue I liked, Dorcas's mother didn't like, but we eventually ended up at a sensible place which was The Monument, the 1820 Settlers Monument, where there was a lovely restaurant and bar facility. All the catering happened there and I said "This is fine. I'm happy, no big deal, whatever you want, let's get it done!"

Of course I had a rip roaring bachelor party in Johannesburg which I'm not going to go into detail about, for obvious reasons, but it was organised by my good friend Rob Smuts. We arrived in Grahamstown for the wedding, and Rob was my best man. We got set up in this little lodge called St Aidan's. The original venue where I really wanted to have the party was at St Aidan's hall. We stayed there, and Dorcas was with her mum and dad and her brothers and family, and they were getting ready on their side. My family had come into Grahamstown and that Friday evening, it was a very typical Grahamstown day, with misty, rainy conditions. It was also my mum's 50th birthday the day of our wedding, so she had to kind of sacrifice a big 50th birthday bash for our wedding. At the time I didn't really understand how important that was and what a sacrifice she had made, but I am very grateful to her for that, and things went well. Our family arrived; my mates arrived; we had a good party that night in Grahamstown.

· • • ● • ●• ● • • ·

The next day, Saturday, was the day of the service. It was an afternoon wedding with an evening reception. We woke up on that Saturday morning, which was still a bit grey and overcast, and we heard the news that the 1820 Settlers Monument had been vandalised and set ablaze during the night. It had been burning the whole night, and of course it had burnt out the wedding venue where we were supposed to have our reception. I couldn't believe it. We rushed around to verify that the story was correct, but we could see that the monument was on fire, smoke billowing out over the top of the mountain. Our day immediately turned into one of full-blown event management services with under five hours to try and change venues. We needed to set everything up, get catering organised for a big wedding of a hundred-odd people in the wedding party and the wedding guests, and it was chaos and we didn't know what to do. So I said to Dorcas's parents "Listen, you look after the bride, we're going to go to the church. If we don't have a fancy reception that's not a problem, but leave it up to me and my family, we'll organise something!"

I rushed in to see the owner of the hotel we were staying at and said "Is this venue available tonight, can we use it?", and they said certainly we could but they had had a huge 21st birthday party there the night before. They told us the place was a mess and that the chef was not there that day. There was no time to lose! My family and I rolled up our sleeves and first had to clean out this hall which was ankle deep in beer cans and cigarette ash from a 21st the night before, it was disgusting. I woke my brother Nigel who is a fully trained chef and told him I needed him. I told him what had happened, and then I told the hotel manager "My brother's in charge of the kitchen. Do what he wants you to do, buy what he wants you to buy, and we'll square you off at the end of it all!" They agreed readily. My brother had to hose down the kitchen and get that all in working order before they could start food preparation. They went into town, bought what they had to buy and it was all hands on deck. Cousins and friends were peeling pumpkins and potatoes and there was plenty of shouting and screaming and chaos, but it was organised chaos. We were even able to type up a menu and get that printed, as well as buy some flowers, lay and decorate the tables. My sister ran around and helped with that, it was a tremendous team effort from our family! Eventually I asked what was going to happen for the Lunn's. Dorcas's mum was not that thrilled with the fact that we were back in the venue that she wasn't happy with, but anyway, they understood, everybody was all smiles and we were almost done. Eventually I had to leave, have a quick shower, get into my wedding outfit, and get to the church.

It was raining and I sat in the front pew as the church filled up. Rob was with me and eventually I realised that Dorcas had arrived, but my family hadn't. I rushed up to the back of the church and I said, "My family haven't arrived yet, please just give them another 5 minutes!" Dorcas got back in the car, and she and her dad drove around for 5 more minutes. Eventually my family arrived in dribs and drabs. They sat down and I remember looking at my brother and my mum's hands which were orange because they couldn't get all the pumpkin stain off their hands. But at last, this beautiful bride walked into the church, we got married before God and all the witnesses, and that's how we started our marriage. We then had an amazing party, with a great meal my brother dished up for us and it was as if nothing had gone wrong.

· · · · ● · ● · · ·

We delivered excellence and a wonderful party, and we drove off into the sunset as it were, on to our honeymoon. It was truly spectacular. We went to India and visited the Taj Mahal, Delhi, Jaipur, Agra, Udaipur, right down the bottom of India to Goya. Next we flew like jet set kings & queens to the Maldives for a week, before returning home after three weeks. It was the most amazing start to our marriage; India had been embedded and implanted in our hearts. Making the decision to get married and moving forward in life was an incredible and life changing event.

Twenty-Seven

New Home, Big move

"Home isn't where you're from, it's where you find light
when all grows dark." - Pierce Brown

ON RETURN FROM THE spectacular honeymoon, it was straight back into
the crazy work life and pace that we had created as a small business. I must
admit I remember the three-week break being a huge benefit to me. It gave
me clarity and a sense of wellbeing that is important, and it was something
that I had forgotten for a long time – to take good, long breaks from the
business environment to sharpen the mind and restore the creativity levels.
Coming back to Johannesburg after a fabulous wedding and a spectacular
honeymoon was wonderful. I looked forward to this new journey of being
in a life partnership with Dorcas, and things were good.

My little bachelor pad in Sunninghill was no longer what it had been
to me, and it seemed like I needed to move on from that. Dorcas and
I started to house-hunt together, to dream together. We dreamed of a
more interesting place to live, of settling down and making our first big
choice together after our marriage. We used to drive around and look at
places within our budget, and every now and again we would cruise into
something that was obviously way, way above our budget. We'd pretend
that we were inheriting big amounts of cash and strut around these huge
mansions in Johannesburg, just to have a look at how the rich and famous
lived.

On one of these occasions we were out quite early on a Sunday morning,
we had one or two places to view that we had picked out from looking in
the Saturday newspaper. We drove through a suburb that was really quite

close to where the office was, rather a comfortable area, and we followed some signs and eventually got to this home in Bryanston, in Lansdown road. We drove in and up this long driveway and thought this looked like quite an interesting place. We walked around and it was obviously way too big for just the two of us, but we dreamed of one day having children and imagined the family running around and playing on the lawn. It was quite a cold day in the middle of winter I remember, and we went through the house and I commented that this was a similar house to that in which I had grown up as a child. It was an old-world kind of house and Dorcas had the same reflection, saying it reminded her also of her family home in Zimbabwe, or Rhodesia as it was then. We looked all around it and decided it had caught our interest.

We decided we were getting a bit hungry and went off to have lunch at one of our favourite spots. It turned into rather a boozy lunch, at Turtle Creek I think it was, and on the way back to Sunninghill, we decided to pop back to Bryanston because we quite fancied this house. Fuelled by a bottle of champagne or whatever we had been drinking, I asked the estate agent how much the property was going for. Of course it was really at the top end of our budget, but I said we liked it. Dorcas and I went outside and lay on the grass together. Dorcas commented that this was the kind of house that we'd like to get. We thought about it and decided yes, it was the sort of place we wanted. We could renovate it and we could do this and that. Anyway, I got a bee in my bonnet that this is what we would do. We looked at our budget, and thought maybe if we got it at a particular price level, we could just about afford it. If we sold my bachelor pad in Sunninghill, and she put in some money from her side, perhaps we could get a decent deposit together and afford a monthly bond.

We put in an offer, met with the seller on Tuesday night and by Wednesday we had a signed and sealed agreement that we were going to buy this house. It was subject to us getting bond approval so we rushed around and got the bond approved, and filled in all the application forms. We needed to sell the bachelor pad, which was a condition of sale. We put the house on the market, and thankfully the market was pretty good at the time, so we got the price that we wanted for it. Before we knew it we were moving into a new house. This new house was on an acre of land, it was absolutely enormous, and I couldn't believe that we had actually gone and taken this massive step to buy a house together in the upmarket suburb of Bryanston.

It was fantastic and we were so excited, and of course with this excitement came a new lease of life on getting a new place and doing it up, it was just tremendous. I remember the day that the original owner, who had built the house, moved out. We looked at this house and thought what have we done? It was so old and there are many crazy things in this home that we need to change. No sooner than the ex-owners were out the door, Dorcas was throwing out some of the things that these people had cherished and tendered. I remember the woman walked back into the house and Dorcas was tossing out her favourite pot plant from one part of the house. That kind of signified that the change had begun. The game was on and we were changing things to suit us, and so began a tremendous experience. Anyway, that house is the home that we still live in today. We've changed it, renovated it in stages and then got to a stage where we felt that in order to really get the value of the house we needed to do something radical. Today we live in an almost brand-new house on the same piece of land. We flattened the original house and had a family friend who is an architect design us a dream home that we built on the existing foundations of the old house. The garden is beautiful, particularly the trees, and every time I drive in through my gate I am so at peace in this place. I feel that it has been God's provision for us, a place to call home and that is such an important thing for me. Travelling around the world as I do, and having businesses in so many different destinations, it's still so important for me to be anchored, to have my home and a place that I love being in. This is a place in which we have so many good times with family and friends, and now with the children. It's a true place of anchoring, my safe harbour that gives me a great sense of peace and a true sense of achievement.

Twenty-Eight
The Big Crash

"Change will not come if we wait for some other person or some other time. We are the ones we've been waiting for. We are the change that we seek." Barack Obama

A FEW MONTHS PASSED and we had been in our new house for about six months or so. I was twenty-nine years old, turning thirty, and it was a big year. So many amazing things happened but unfortunately the biggest event of that year was the crash of the Logans business. Logans had been flying high with their low-cost carrier airline business, but they had really been running out of control in terms of growth. They couldn't manage the cash-flow and the cash requirements of this new business venture into the airline industry. The long and short of it was that a local travel agency distribution network got wind of this pending failure, and they instructed all their young travel agents around the country to no longer book with Logans Tours. That had an immediate impact of obviously cutting off the final revenue stream and cash generating opportunities for this business and the inevitable happened. Logans Tours went into bankruptcy, or liquidation.

I remember the days prior to that decision, Russell and Colin were frantically running around the country trying to find other investors, trying to sell the business, trying to rope people in to rescue them and it was rather sad. The staff knew very little about what was coming, and I can't even remember exactly how it was finally announced, but Russell and Colin sheepishly told people that the business was closing, the bank was foreclosing and there were all sorts of legal cases pending. I think people got half their salary and were told that was it. It was devastating news.

To top it all, the tourists that the company left stranded around the world became front page news of the Sunday Times. It was hugely talked about on radio, television and in newspapers. I remember just being in this completely numb zone wondering how I was going to rescue my business out of this. I was a company that was operating independently, but still with co-shareholders, and of course I was fighting for survival. There was so much money that was owed to me. I found out that during my absence on one of my trips to an international trade show, money out of my account had been used to prop up their ailing business and I wasn't able to get it all back by the time things folded.

There was almost a million rand owing to my business at the time. That money didn't really belong to me; it was money that was held on deposit from one of my major clients and I was not going to be able to get this back. The panic, the feeling of overwhelming dread was unbearable. I remember going into the garden and retching, almost vomiting at the nauseating anxiousness that this moment had caused. My friends were nowhere to be seen. I didn't know where they were, I couldn't talk to them, they were running and hiding and dodging reporters, and I was trying to keep my team together and focused through this chaos. At the time my dad actually called me up and said "I hear there's big trouble, how are you, and do you need any help?" and I said, "Yes, there's a lot of trouble, please Dad can we meet? I need some advice." It was very sobering going from riding high to now needing help from Daddy again. The bottom line is that yeah, I needed help, and thank God for my family. My dad was a really strong supporter, he never once said 'I told you so' or anything like that. He just said he was very proud of what I had achieved, and that we would look at the situation from all angles and get through it together. We were able to utilise his network of legal help and professional services from audit firms, and his banking connections to get the best advice we could and to move forward.

I had my 30th birthday party planned, I had invited a few people and it was a big deal turning 30 and being severely in debt. I said to my buddy Rob I couldn't believe it, I had turned 30 and I was millions of rand in debt rather than being a millionaire, which had been the goal. Collectively between my new bond, the business money that had been removed, my car and other commitments, I was nearly two million rand in debt. That was a shocking weight of indebtedness and a scary position. On reflection, the worst part of it wasn't the money, it was the relationship that broke and the sense of betrayal. It was the end of something that was so good from a friendship point of view, and it was just being left to hang out and dry. In the negotiations, having taken the advice from various people, I was advised to liquidate the company alongside everybody else and start again. I said to the legal guys and accounting guys that this wasn't a path that I wanted to follow. I believed that the South African corporate community was a small one and that that kind of approach would just jeopardise my future. I chose not to liquidate and do what seemed to be regular business practice. I chose instead to honour my debts and to work my way out of it all.

That was a huge moral decision to make the right call and to get on with things. It was one of those moments where I look back on a tremendous amount of pain, and of pressure to make a decision that was maybe an easier route out, but I chose stubbornly to do the right thing, and I don't regret that. It was three years of exceptionally hard labour to get out of that debt position and onto the straight and narrow again, but the one thing that I do treasure is that I was able to look at myself in the mirror and say that I had made the right call, that I operated with integrity in the situation.

One of the funny or crazy stories out of that time is that I was harassed by a Radio 702 reporter for my part of the story. I said "Listen, I don't really know what was going on, I don't know who was responsible for what, I've got my own business and I am carrying on and I don't want to speak any more than that because I don't really know!" She persisted in hounding me and following me, and I ran and got in my car. Under the pressure and stress of all this I was worried that I might have a fit and just needed to get out and escape. She followed me in her car and eventually the only safe place I could think of was my doctor Mark Oliver's waiting room. I burst into the reception area and I said that I needed to see Mark urgently. I rushed into his room and I babbled, "Mark this has happened, and I've got a reporter following me, I'm so stressed out and please can you just hide me somewhere!" He put me down in one of his rooms, closed the door and went out to speak to the reporter. He chased her away, and then came back and gave me a sedative and told me to chill out. I don't know how long I was there for, but it just seemed a place of safety and a place that I needed to be in for a little while to unwind. I'm always grateful to Mark for protecting me in that way. It was a funny story that wasn't funny at all, it was deeply disturbing. I remember being in tears many, many evenings after that. The hurt, the pain and the betrayal of the friendship was, and still is today after twenty years, so painful to think about.

Although Russell and I have come to terms again, and it's not as painful now as it was then, it was a devastating time. Thinking about that period, I also need to thank the people in my team at the time who believed that we could get through it and believed me when I said we have the ability to deliver excellence. We were able to retain our customers and that was a good news story. We could perform and be creative to come out of the devastation. Some very strong people rallied around me and that vision we co created was a powerful one. It was a monumental team effort including the effort of my father and my wife. Both of their most important contributions were that they kept on believing in me, kept on talking positive words over me and my life. Told me they knew I could do it, that I knew I could do it. My dad said not to worry about the finances, that I should go out and do what I did best, which was selling. He encouraged me to go and talk to my customers, to make sure that I was out there promoting and selling. He promised to take care of the back office and the finances while I did the rest. I was so grateful for that because it allowed me to get up every day and put on a brave face, to hit the road and knock on doors and relentlessly pound the pavements until we found enough work. It was this baptism of fire that produced so many incredible positives as I reflect on it.

As we started off this part of the story, we had just bought a house and Dorcas and I were a young newly wed couple . We had only just got married and there was a huge sense of this new partnership and the great responsibility that goes with it. The other dynamic of this partnership, in this moment of intense crisis, was the stability and support of my wife. My wife works for Woolworths and has worked for the same company for 30 years. Her career has always progressed and advanced, with promotion after promotion after promotion. She has been the stable income earner in our family when I wasn't able to pay for things myself, and she had enough money to cover and support both of us. Being in a dynamic marriage, where an entrepreneur and a corporate person came together to fight the challenges of life, was and is an incredible story. It still happens today, the support, the strength, the commitment. I remember the tenderness, being able to collapse in her lap and sob when I needed to and then to be gently told to get up and go. To be told not to give up, to never give up, and that we could do it together was an incredible thing that happened very early in our marriage. That early experience, and that commitment to struggling through tough things together, helps us even today. We can overcome any challenge, no matter how big or small, as long as we are together.

Twenty-Nine
Advice, Values & Decisions to Overcome

"Being challenged in life is inevitable, being defeated is optional." – Roger Crawford

THE FINANCIAL FALL OF Logans Tours was very nearly the end of this small beginning that I had made as the Uwin Iwin business. At the time it was possibly one of the most remarkable opportunities to display a set of values and decisions that went contrary to some highly intelligent business advice from some really trusted advisors. I mentioned earlier that my dad got involved and we went off to see his auditor at the time, Kessel Feinstein. Frank, who was a senior partner at the time, was a really trusted advisor of my dad. Frank listened very carefully, he looked at the situation and he was tremendously empathetic, but he said maybe we need to contain the risk, contain the loss, and liquidate and start again. But he said that before we did this, we should cover our bases and seek some legal advice. We went off to Edward Nathan Sonnenburg, today ENS Africa, paid the fees, and also received similar advice. We were told this kind of thing happens, and the best way of sorting it out was to fold the whole thing and carry on. I was adamant that I didn't want to taint my reputation as a young entrepreneur, nor did I want to be responsible for taking money from someone, albeit a giant corporation. I didn't want to lose that money, because somebody would have to be accountable for it at the end of the day. I was prepared to stand up, take accountability and make sure that we paid this money back. I wanted to prove that we were good despite the circumstances.

I had long discussions with my father, and my father was very supportive of this direction. I remember one thing that he said to me: "David, you must know that this is a hard path that you are going to choose, and it's not going to be easy, but if we stand together we will work through it." Again I want to say out loud that I was just so grateful for my father's support in the middle of tremendous adversity. So I said "Dad, we've got to get these guys out, we've got to make a way of getting 100% ownership of this business!" We started phoning around and eventually I was able to get Russell and Colin telephonically. I talked to them and my suggestion was that they sign over their shares for the token value of one rand. I wanted them to relinquish their ownership of that equity and let me take on 100% of the debts, so I could attempt to reengineer and resuscitate the business. But it wasn't to be that simple, and this is where I certainly felt that the knife went deep into my heart. Not only had these guys completely screwed me by taking this money out of my bank and then being reckless with their own business, but they then demanded a payment of R25000 each for their equity, where clearly, we were in debt, bankrupt, and without too much prospect. They explained it away by telling me if I thought the business was only worth one rand, then I should fold like everyone else, but as I clearly saw value in the business then they wanted their share.

I was so angry, and so betrayed, but eventually we came up with the money, paid them, and got our shares signed over. It was very, very bittersweet. I had tasted the cold steel of ruthlessness. There was absolutely no sweetness other than the fact that somewhere in my head I knew that I owned 100% of the business. 100% of what you might ask – 100% of a lot of debt and hardship to pay this money back when effectively I was on my own. But the decision to overcome these challenges was deeply embedded in my soul, and my focus was so determined. I was determined not to be overwhelmed, not to be overcome. I had to prove to myself, and the world, and certainly to these guys that had inflicted the pain that I was better than them and I was better than the circumstances of doing it and just going with the flow. I had to show that my decision to be counterintuitive would develop into something and I could go through the tough moments and overcome them.

The next thing I had to do was negotiate this debt issue with this money that was on deposit. I went off to the big German motor manufacturing company, to see the directors. I set up an appointment to tell them that the money was no longer there. I arrived at their big head office and I was almost frogmarched into a boardroom where there were some very grumpy looking senior directors of this business staring at me. I remember the managing director of the business was also there, I had never met him before but he was getting involved, and he asked me to please explain the situation. I carefully told them about the company setup and what had happened, and how the money had gone missing. I was then asked what I was going to do about it. I said I would pay everything back but I needed time. I wanted to pay the debt back to the business over a three-year period and was committed to doing that. With this suggestion the managing director went absolutely wild. He started shouting, screaming and banging his hands on the desk. He stated the obvious that they weren't a bank and they weren't in the habit of lending money to little businesses like mine. Anyway, there was a finance guy, later I learned that he was the treasurer of the business, who asked me to leave the room. He obviously calmed the managing director down, they had an internal conversation and then they all came storming out of the boardroom.

I was sitting like a naughty schoolboy outside the headmaster's office, the stress levels were huge and I really thought I was going to be arrested or something like that, that's how much of a fraud I felt. Anyway, this treasurer guy took me to his office, sat me down and said he wanted me to come back with a plan of how exactly I was going to pay it back. The only thing that they were going to be prepared to do is take six bank-guaranteed cheques payable every six months until the capital balance was repaid. He said they would discount these negotiable instruments with a discounting house, bring the cash back into their balance sheet and effectively I would owe the bank that bought the instruments the money, and not their business. I sort of understood what he was saying, and what he wanted, so I left. I remember the drive; I remember getting into my car and almost collapsing over the steering wheel in tears. I just didn't know how I could possibly come up with that kind of a structure. I drove back to Jo'burg and went to see my father. We sat down together, I recounted the whole meeting and he agreed to try and help me. We went and saw his bankers so that we understood exactly what this whole deal meant, and the following day I took six bank-guaranteed cheques with me to Pretoria and delivered them to the business. They were very grateful, and I asked them please to help me with these repayments, to continue to do business with me and support me. They assured me they would but of course that was the last time I ever got business from that company!

Again, that was another very hard lesson, but one that I fully understand. The reality of those days was that I was now effectively indebted to my father and that if I couldn't produce the profits and returns, over the next three years, I would have left him with a hole in his bank account. In one way that upped the ante for me even more, and the thought of failing my father who had always supported me was as enormous as anything I could think of. Instead of blind fear, it fuelled my fire, it increased my determination to succeed and get on with things. It's not to say for one minute that I wasn't anxious or fearful because I most certainly was, but I was able, for most of the time anyway, to keep that under check, to keep focused and go for it. I think the moment where I was weakest was when the emotional impact of loss of friendship, absolute bewilderment that a friend would do that to me, and the overwhelming task all kind of merged and I doubted myself. That's when the tears came and the fears overwhelmed me, but that's when my wife stepped in, and my dad too and they just reassured me that they were going to be there no matter what. Even if we failed, we would still look after each other and that is something that I will always be grateful for.

Thirty

The Call

"God does not choose people because of their ability, but because of their availability." - Brother Andrew

DURING THIS DARK TIME, something quite miraculous happened. This is really when I had an incredible spiritual awakening. I know hypocrites always say religion is a crutch for the weak, but I don't believe that. A relationship with God is not for weak people at all, it's for people who are strong. But in amongst this adversity I got a phone call and it was actually from a competitor, this guy Eugene De Villiers, who owned a competitive incentive company called The Extra Mile Company. He was a larger than life charismatic individual who was almost a pioneer of incentive travel in the South African industry. Eugene phoned me and said "Ah, hi Dave, it's Eugene, how are you doing?" and I said I was okay. He then said, "You know what, I phoned you because this morning when I was praying, God told me to phone you and tell you that He loves you." My reaction was a stunned silence. Then I responded in a rather cocky arrogant way, and said "Eugene, what are you smoking, man? Thanks, I appreciate that..." or something like that. Eugene then asked if I believed, and if I went to church. I told him I was a believer but I hadn't been to church for a long time, so thanks but no thanks, that kind of thing. So he graciously hung up and this thought went through my head "What, guys talk to God, God talks back to them, really? This is crazy!" Anyway, I got on with my busy day.

• • • ● • ● • ● • • •

I think it was seven or eight days later, Eugene phoned me again. "Dave, hi how are you doing?" "Yeah, I'm fine thanks Eugene, how are you doing?" He then said, "I'm fine, but I woke up this morning, I had my prayer time and God impressed on my heart to phone you, and just again tell you that He loves you so much." This time he caught me at a moment where the emotions were high and I thanked Eugene and told him I was going through a tough time. He told me he knew and that he was thinking of me. He asked if there was anything he could do to help and then suggested I come to church. I told him that I had just got married and my wife was Catholic, and every now and again I went to the Catholic church with her, even though it was basically just to take her to church. Eugene said that was fine but suggested we come along to their church in Lonehill. I got the address and said maybe I would go and of course I didn't.

• • • ● • ● • ● • • •

I got invited to an industry get-together at the Sandton Sun, it was an event to showcase some of their new properties and I went along. Eugene was there. I remember him coming over to me and telling me he had a really good idea, and that he wanted to talk to me, so we set up a meeting for some time the following week. In the middle of a crazy survival kind of day, I headed out to his place. It was quite a drive as he lived out on a smallholding just north of Fourways, and I drove out there in the hope that he had a business proposition for me. I was thinking maybe we could merge or team up, maybe he could help me, maybe there was some way of doing a joint venture; this was what was in my mind. Anyway, I drove out there wondering how I should position this current situation, really deeply ingrained in the cut and thrust of making a deal or a proposal or something like that.

I got out there and went into this huge, oversized living room and we sat down and had coffee. I was sitting on a sofa, there was a huge coffee table in between us and he was sitting on the other side of the table. Eugene said to me "Dave, you know, I've brought you out here and I just wanted to tell you it's not a business idea that I'm going to be talking to you about, I want to talk to you about God." And I just imploded, I freaked out. I said, "What do you mean you want to talk about God, I've come out here to talk about business! Do you know how busy I am, you know the crisis that I'm in, I've been screwed over, made 101 business mistakes, I've lost a lot of money, I'm in debt..." and eventually the tears just came, and I had what is probably the closest to having a nervous breakdown as I ever have. I just couldn't take it anymore, I was so angry, and I was teary, and it was just a mess. He got such a fright, he backed down and apologised but I said I didn't want to hear about it. I was screaming and shouting and saying I didn't want to hear about this religious nonsense. I was really ranting and raving. He said again that he was sorry and told me to calm down. He gave me a tissue and brought me some tea. Then he said that before I left, he just wanted to read one thing from the Bible. So, I almost started screaming again, but I just said, "Oh whatever, read it."

Eugene opened the Bible, went to Psalms, and read Psalm 23 from the Psalms of David, and it's the very famous psalm, that starts with "The Lord Is My Shepherd, I shall not be in want...", and as he read this to me I felt this unbelievable, overwhelming presence which I now know is the presence of God, the Holy Spirit, and I felt this touch, this physical touch on my chest. Now bearing in mind he was sitting at least 5m away from me, I was startled when I felt this touch on my chest and I didn't know what was going on. I just kept on weeping and weeping, and he finished the Psalm, and then he sat there in silence. I sat there too, and he asked what had happened. I said I didn't know what happened, but I just felt God touch me, so he asked me to tell him about it. I said I didn't know what to say, but I knew that God had just spoken to me and I didn't know what to do. Eugene said "Well, do you want to give your life to Jesus?" I said, "Yes! How do I do that?" He told me to say a prayer after him, and the prayer went along the lines of "God I am sorry I have ignored You for so long. I thank You for showing yourself to me and I want to turn away from my wicked ways and embrace You and ask You to come into my heart. Lord Jesus, I believe that You died for my sins, and that I want Your help, I need Your help, I need to submit to You Lord, and I want You to be in my life, like You were in the life of David in the Psalms." And again, I felt this overwhelming touch from God. It was indescribable; it was a sense of energy and exhilaration, a deep sense of peace and joy. Hope had returned into my life, and I knew that God was going to help me find a way through this.

· · · ●· ● ● · ·

I drove off feeling as if I had overcome in that moment; that the victory had been won. God had opened a way and yet I was still deeply in the middle of a crisis obviously, and had many years of working this thing out, but I sensed that with God on my side it was possible. This awakening, this encounter, this experience of God's touch in my life, it was astounding. I don't know many people that have had that physical touch. I know people have experienced God in different ways, but I sneaked off to church because I didn't know how my wife was going to cope with this different non-Catholic experience. I went off to church on my own, to where Eugene went to church at this Jesus centred, bible-based non-denominational type of church. I remember walking in there and feeling quite strange. I sat at the back and the singing and the worship started, and I quite enjoyed that. Then this guy got up and he preached, and I felt like someone had shared with him my deepest, innermost secrets and needs. Every word that he spoke I felt was directed straight at me. Again, I felt that overwhelming sense of God's presence and touch, and again I wept, and yet there was this peace and this joy and I knew that I was in the right place. I kept returning and Eugene helped me understand and interpret what was going on, and things just went from strength to strength in my own faith.

I then got the courage to share that with my wife and asked her to come along and see for herself what this church was about. Reluctantly she came and joined one Sunday, and had an incredible experience of God's presence and love. We have now been part of that church for over twenty five years. We have had an incredible journey of faith, and learning, of understanding and reading the Bible, of knowing and experiencing an understanding of the Old and the New Testament, and it has been amazing. It's such a part of who I am now. My faith is embedded in my DNA and looking back on those moments in time I can only say, with absolute reverence and respect, that there was an abundance of hard work and great effort, but miraculous things happened along the way that were clearly God's provision, doors of opportunity opened when they needed to and I was able to make every single payment exactly on time, not sooner, not later, but on time. A cheque and a payment got made so that that cheque and that debt could clear without impacting on my father.

It's such a good story, it's actually such a wonderful story and my gratitude in my heart to my God is eternal. I couldn't have done it without Him, I don't want to do it without Him, and I'm grateful that both my wife and I were baptised and regularly have incredible God encounters, where God just lifts our spirits. He joins us together and gives us hope and a sense of direction and purpose that is significant and spirit led. I've come to realise that it's not only for me that that experience happened, and for my family and my own well-being, but I've been able to share and encourage other people, so many other people along the way, in a similar way that Eugene helped me and pointed me towards God.

· · · ●·● ● · ·

I want my story to also be a story of God's greatness and love, and it's a big reason for writing this book. It's because I want to share with other people and other entrepreneurs, and people that are facing adversity and struggles and tough times that God is so real, and God cares. It's not only about the tough times. God is in the joyful moments, and makes the joyful moments so much richer, so much more abundant. No matter how successful a person is or not, we have incredible access to a spiritual world, to the life of our Lord Jesus Christ and that is wonderful.

Thirty-One
Kicked Out

"If all you can do is crawl, start crawling." - Rumi

Part of the fallout of the disaster that came upon Logans Tours is that we co-shared an office lease. We were trying to keep going and negotiate with the landlord that we could continue to rent our little part of the building, but they were having none of it. We were given notice and effectively kicked out. We had to go and find a new home for the business. So, we went out, scouted around and I came across a letting agent, Alistair Barclay, who was a very interesting guy. Alistair and I got on quite well, and he found us a property in a building complex I think he owned, in Wessels Rd, Rivonia. It was a couple of blocks down from where we were, and we moved in and started again.

It was quite a significant and important step for us, to move out of the old, and set up something new. It created an iconic start for us again, and we configured the office the way we wanted it. I had quite a nice little office, an open-plan area and an accounts office. It was very simple, but nice and professional, and so we got on with things. I remember my dad would come in in the morning and he used to say "Don't worry about the bank or the money, go out and sell. Sell, sell, sell, you're good at that and that's what we need. I'll save the money and manage it properly. You just go and get the new revenue." So that's what I did. I hit the pavements and the phones and off I went. I was also obviously now praying a great deal every day and regularly popping into friends for encouragement and advice. We would make connections and try to tap other peoples' networks.

Thirty-Two

Wessels Road Climb Out

"Begin today. Declare out loud to the universe that you are willing to let go of struggle and eager to learn through joy." - Sarah Ban Breathnach

WESSELS ROAD WAS THE beginning of the climb out for us, and as I mentioned earlier, we would secure new clients just in time, they would pay us deposits and we would be able to get off and do our thing again. I had just the most fantastic team of people. With all of that going on, I don't think I had one single person abandon ship. They all said they were staying; they were going to help ride it out. They truly were amazing people that were just there, always willing to give it a go. Looking back I don't think that was a tremendous leadership process, but rather the result of being committed to a dream. A vision is contagious, it's infectious, and people that want to come along will endure some incredibly tough stuff together with you to help achieve the dream. Of course, you always have to ensure there is great communication. You must pay careful attention to being grateful, to recognising, rewarding and encouraging people along the way as they battle it out with you in the trenches.

All this time I was waking up every morning and heading out to work with a mission. I needed to make sure that I didn't fall foul of meeting the payments to the bank every 6 months, and that we maintained our existing service levels to customers. Equally important was the fact that we started to grow and develop new customer relations through a very aggressive sales process. I would prospect almost every day, getting on the road every day in my car, seeing different people, creating new opportunities and every now and again winning a new deal which was a tremendous relief. This was also a tremendous challenge from the perspective of having to take on board a new client, with the existing infrastructure. We were not able to spend any money on new staffing and keeping a team together and focused was a tremendous leadership challenge.

• • • ●• ● ●• • •

I remember my dad would remind me on a regular basis to play to my strengths, get out there and do what I did best. He would say I was the rainmaker for the business, and he would take care of administering the finances. The cash flow was always tight, we managed that very effectively; and slowly but surely we started building our way out of a very difficult situation. We had survived the stigma of being associated with a business that had been liquidated. We seemed to have passed through, although we had several competitors that used to remind us and even sometimes in a pitch situation remind clients! I got very annoyed with that, it had nothing to do with them and it certainly didn't have anything to do with us. I remember phoning a competitor once, as I had heard that he had bad-mouthed us to a client. I was very straight up and down and blunt with this guy, and I said something along the lines of if he was going to play dirty like that, he had picked on the wrong guy. I asked in no uncertain terms that that would never happen again, and I don't think it did. As time moved by, less of those kinds of reports and incidents happened, but it took tremendous courage and perseverance to make it through.

• • • ●• ● ●• • •

Miraculously along the way, God opened up deals and payments and things that were just so timeous. I remember we were facing one of the six-monthly payment requirements to the bank, and it looked rather bleak as there wasn't anything big on the horizon in terms of invoicing coming in. Then a client phoned me up and said, "It's the end of our budgeting cycle, and we've got this extra money in our budget that we need to spend – please invoice me for quite a substantial amount of money." I couldn't believe it, it was absolutely miraculous. I was able to invoice for the money, we were able to be judicious in having enough money to cover the client's needs and we were able to make the payment. There were many, many things along the way that I couldn't ascribe to my own personal intelligence, cleverness, or courage. They were just little miracles that I was witnessing along the way and I couldn't wait to get to church on Sundays to give thanks to God for His provisions.

· · · · ● · ● · ● · ·

There were also moments of deep sadness still, of losing a dear friend, and going through that leadership challenge. I was sometimes feeling very isolated and alone and I thank God for a tremendous partner in my wife, who was always by my side and understood the challenges. We were very encouraged by the way we were moving forward and through to the next phase. We were building and climbing out of a very deep hole. I remember three odd years in, we had made that final repayment and I had freed myself of the indebtedness of the past. At that moment a tremendous weight came off my shoulders. I always strive and would encourage others to first seek and then find independence and freedom from debt. It is such a massive psychological burden to be lugging around every single day, and it is so easy to get into debt.

Of course, the kind of debt that I was in was a debt that I didn't engineer myself, but I certainly could have done things to avoid it had I been more in control of the finances. I take full accountability for that, but it's the other sorts of debt, housing debt, motor car debt, credit card debt, that people strain under. It's so difficult to describe the pressure, but the pressure is relieved when one can pay off everything and be debt-free from a business perspective; it was certainly marvellous. We were able to start investing in people and processes and up our game, and that development for us was a huge thing. For me it was so mixed up with my faith and my journey of belief, belief in God above, and also the belief in myself, in the talents that He had created that moved and navigated me through the stormy waters of very, very difficult times.

Thirty-Three
Lonehill Village Church/ LHVC

"You are never left alone when you are alone with God."
- Woodrow Kroll

THE LONEHILL VILLAGE CHURCH was an incredible place and still is for me today. It had a massive impact on my life and my journey with God, my understanding of the Bible and how to live a life really of my calling, with the LHVC. It's a small Christian church where I became born-again. I came to understand the true nature of my salvation, and what Jesus had done for me on the cross, at a very personal level. I started going there on Sundays, really getting involved with the community, and early on I was roped into helping others. Being engaged in the church and engaged in a ministry where you're not just sitting warming a pew every Sunday, your faith becomes a practical faith, a faith which is lived. I have a huge amount of thanks and respect for my little local village church for giving me that.

The very first activity that my wife and I got involved with, from a ministry point of view, was getting trained up as leaders, and then participating in and running the Alpha Training Course. This is a training course that was put together out of an Anglican background from a church in the UK, Holy Trinity Brompton, by a pastor named Nicky Gumble. This course has gone worldwide and exposed many Christians to a deeper understanding of faith, and it has also reached many, many other non-Christians and helped them make a decision as to whether they wanted to follow Jesus or not.

The course is still run today, and over four million people have been on Alpha Courses. They are effectively small courses that are run with a twenty-minute video introduction, then after listening to the video small groups of people get to ask difficult questions or questions about faith that have never been asked before. I must say, just being involved and listening to the material also deepened my understanding of the Faith. Having to be the one that answers some of those tough questions also stretched my wife and I quite a bit. We loved being actively involved in promoting the Gospel, and we had tremendous experiences along the way, where God just gives you the wisdom to be gentle and loving and to answer tough questions. You need to work alongside God and see how the Holy Spirit ministers and opens up and brings about healing and wholeness to people who really need it.

Towards the end of the course, you go away for a night or two on what's called The Holy Spirit Weekend, where the teaching is all about the work of the Holy Spirit. Very often when you're going through these weekends, there's a tremendous outpouring of the Holy Spirit's love and presence at those workshops. Just to have seen healing, to have seen this great tenderness that God pours out on people, to meet them at the very point where they most need help, I must say deepened my own faith immensely. We ran about four or five Alpha courses as Alpha Course leaders and it very much provided a solid foundation for both Dorcas and I for our faith. I certainly would encourage anyone who hasn't been on an Alpha Course to get onto one, but not only that, I would also encourage you to try and get into leadership in your local community and church.

Besides the Alpha Course, there was another key dimension of building our faith and being able to walk through really tough times, both in the business and on a personal level. We were encouraged early on to get involved in what we call home fellowships. Small groups of believers meet sometime during the week, usually on a Wednesday night. The groups pray for each other, do a bit of praise and worship, and look at either a bit of the scripture or review the sermon that was preached on Sunday. They look into how that applies or can be applied into everyday living. I think those building blocks in our faith were wonderful and again, I give great encouragement to anybody that wants to walk a strong walk, to be surrounded by Christians who care, meet regularly and are serious about their faith. Today we are still actively involved. We went from participating to leading our own fellowship group quite early on and will continue to do that as a really important expression of our faith.

Another admirable part of the village church was its leader. He was a very humble but highly learned and degreed man, Dr Chris Peppler. He has three doctorates and was also the foundation or founding principle of the South African online theological college. Chris was given a vision early on, a concept of a small church. I suppose he could have quite easily built a bigger and bigger congregation over the many years, and had a massive church, but that wasn't what God's calling was on his life. He put his ego aside in order to run a small church, and when the congregation reached a certain number, the church would then fund and support what they would call a church plant, where a number of congregants went off to a new location and started a new small church. This is a very difficult thing to do successfully, but one that really has worked in keeping the community of believers in an intimate relationship with each other and with God.

I am tremendously thankful for the spiritual mentorship of Dr Peppler and all of those involved with Eldership and leadership at the LHVC. This is really a tremendous part of my life where I give real glory and thanks to God for the call. Of course when my children came along, and that's another story entirely as to how God provided for us for children, not in the conventional way, but where we adopted children, these adopted children also came to be loved and accepted and find a wonderful place within the body of believers attending Sunday school. They are growing up within this community of friends and believers. It is a place of refuge, a place of great strength and inspiration, and a place where service to God and service to His kingdom is so open to anyone that really wants to get involved and engaged.

Thirty-Four

SITE: Society for Incentive Travel Excellence

"Cultural differences should not separate us from each other, but rather cultural diversity brings a collective strength that can benefit all of humanity" by Robert Alan.

MY EARLY INDUSTRY MENTOR, Eugene De Villiers, encouraged me early on to get involved in an association of our industry that was a global association, called SITE. There is a local chapter in South Africa. SITE was the Society of Incentive Travel Excellence, a good place for ongoing education and development of an international network of like-minded individuals. I joined the local chapter and got actively involved, and eventually got nominated to the local board. I really enjoyed the local network as well as attending some of the international conferences. Attending an international conference was really like a vacation with an education slant, and there were some tremendous opportunities that I got. To travel to Thailand, and what they used to call the SITE University, was my first experience of that. There were many other international conferences that I went to, including Toronto in Canada, a place in Merida in Mexico, universities in Orlando, Argentina, Europe and Dubai. These conferences were an excellent place to bond and develop and grow the connectivity, as well as an opportunity to get out of day to day operations and think more strategically. I was eventually nominated onto the South African Board, and then became the president of the South African chapter. Little did I know that my involvement with SITE would, in time, take me onto the international board but that's another story. For me, SITE has certainly played a tremendous role in my business because it's always given me that breathing space to think strategically and to connect internationally. It allows me to transact and do business dealings with other members, and to really establish a home and identity for the discipline that we are in. I relished all my experiences, both at a local and international level.

Thirty-Five

Digital Revolution

"The digital revolution is almost as disruptive to the traditional media business as electricity was to the candle business." - Ken Auletta

THE DIGITAL REVOLUTION ERA occurred roughly between the years of 1997 and 2001. It was a period of extreme growth in the usage and adoption of the Internet by business users and consumers. During this period many internet-based companies, commonly referred to as 'dot coms', were founded and many failed. The whole bubble occurred in the late nineties when there was a rapid rise in the equity markets, fuelled by investment in internet-based companies. Guys were getting multi-millions of dollars for Internet ideas that investors were throwing huge amounts of money at. Of course, many of them failed or lost a huge amount of shareholder value, because they were built on models that weren't sustainable. Their predictions of growth were just unrealistic.

· · · ● · ● · · ·

This digital revolution was in any event of great relevance for Uwin Iwin, and for me as a young entrepreneur. This was the environment in which we were seeing the rise of a new type of business, a new type of industry, and it was very exciting to read the business case studies and the business buzz at the time. I was swept up in the enthusiasm of all of this and thought this could be the way to make it big, to make millions and expand a global business. So many entrepreneurs, including myself at the time, were diving in and having the first stab at this internet or digital revolution. I wanted to know how I could get on this bandwagon and make plenty of money. I remember reading anything I could to find about this new revolutionary digital technology, and I kept on asking myself "What could we do, what could we do?" I was asking friends and people that knew way more about technology than I did what I could do, and where I could find the gap.

The most solid piece of advice came from my university friend our now chairman, Gordon Fraser, who had begun a steady rise in the ranks of Microsoft South Africa. He himself was involved in an entrepreneurial business and decided that he wanted to get a more grounded career in established technology. Microsoft was, and still is, a leader. His advice to me was not to look at finding a new kind of business, but rather to look at how this new type of technology could empower our existing business and add greater value to our customers with digital tools, digital technology and Internet enablement. I remember after that brief conversation being quite deflated in a way that there wasn't an easy mechanism. His advice wasn't to jump stream but rather to see how one could improve the value proposition for customers within our own stream.

· · · · ● · ● · · · ·

Waking up the next day I kept on mulling this around in my head, and just couldn't stop thinking about it. I then had a further conversation with Gordon, and I asked him how to define exactly what this tool was, and what digital tools were in general. We boiled it all down to this: 'It is a highly, highly effective communication tool'. I started looking at my business again, thinking how well this was suited to our type of business where we concentrated on inspiring people and motivating communities! So much of the art of what we do is communication, how you communicate, how you communicate in an inspirational way, the speed at which you communicate, the speed at which you can bring efficiency into the communication channel. Look at this simple example: In the past one used to mail out communication, via the postal service, and suddenly the easy way of doing that was via email, so that was a huge transformational step up in communication. It was just so much faster and so much more effective. You could get a message out, but even better you could get a response with so much more speed and efficiency. So that was one of the dynamics.

The other dynamic was that people were starting to get a little bit more real time feedback in the communication process. Digitisation helped people not only communicate but also understand where they stood as a participant, as a loyal customer, as a potential high performing employee. We looked at our business from a communication or a digitisation perspective. We believed that we could add value to our customer and our participant communities with digital technologies, and so the journey began. Starting with a simple understanding of what internet and digital technologies meant, we began to see how we could now infuse this into our value proposition. All of a sudden, I became exceptionally excited because the passion that I had started off with I knew could be closely aligned and reinvented, using these technologies that were now available.

• • • ● • ● • ● • •

In 1999, we developed the very first version of this technology that we today call NetUwin.com. This was the term or the name that we started with, and we have now had seven generations of this technology. Each generation was designed with multiple levels of improvement and functionality and integration abilities. Back in the day when we started, I was not a pure coding guy, so I had to find some guys who could code, build websites, technology and databases. We started to map out what I believed to be the value-add proposition to a customer, based on an understanding of our industry, the processes, and what needed to be done.

I discovered a new talent, and this was the ability to map a digital solution in a business understanding in layman's terms. I could then relate this to highly technical people and show them a vision of what needed to be produced. The techies or propeller heads as I call them would then scurry off to their glowing screens, sit in dark rooms, eat pizza and drink Coca-Cola all night and then come back the next day with something cool that kind of worked. We would then look at this thing and maybe add an idea, then see what part of the map it then fulfilled. Then we would build the next piece and the next piece until we had a functional picture of what I had in my mind.

That talent that I discovered in myself was then honed through multiple successes and failures. I tried this, tried that, tested it out with a customer, and today it's been developed into a very well-known silicon-valley business approach. This is the lean start-up model where you test something with a customer, you see what works, you eliminate what doesn't, you pivot, you design, you redesign. You keep shaping it around the customer's needs until you find something that is suitable for them, it makes commercial sense and they're willing to part with money for the idea.

· · · · ●· ● ·· ·

So that journey started in 1999 and I like to claim, although I may be proved wrong, that Uwin Iwin was the first to launch a digital point banking system. This was linked in with a catalogue that superseded and surpassed the existing models of reward catalogues that were produced in a coffee table booklet form. People would be sent these coffee table books and brochures of rewards, and then they would gather their rewards. They would be sent their point update via mail, and once they had reached the required target, they could order their chosen reward by faxing in an order form.

We were disruptive in introducing a technology platform to the market, our first version of our online point banking and loyalty programme, and we've kept on building on that. Many other companies around the world were thinking in a similar vein, and in a couple of months that unique window, that we held open for a few months, closed. We could no longer claim to be the only ones and started to become one of many. Today there are many, many software platforms and models available, but none that I know of that have lasted since 1999, years of tech development, of learning, of scaling within a business where it is bespoke, home grown and applied in multiple countries. It is now cloud based and still relevant today, because we are constantly developing and integrating new technologies, new coding languages and so on to produce what is relevant and current in today's market.

· · · ● · ● · ● · · ·

That was the huge journey that we went on from a tech point of view and there are many, many people that I need to acknowledge and thank for helping me on that road to the future. The key architect from a tech point of view was a young guy I met who was about 19 years old. Stuart Higgs was a self-styled, self-taught tech development specialist and he is still with us today as our group CIO and chief technology architect. Stuart and I have been together for many years and we know each other very well. We know what we can do and can't do together, and we are able to build things for a customer's needs extremely quickly and leverage on all of those years of experience of how to do it right, what pitfalls to avoid and how to go really fast. That relationship with Stuart I am exceptionally grateful for, he is an amazing man with massive experience under his belt and many years still to go. He has developed a much wider skill set than just technology. His leadership skills, his management, his business skills have developed substantially and his ethics and his values have always been top draw and incredibly valuable to me and our business.

· · · ● ●· ● ● · ·

The other guy that I am incredibly grateful for is a man called Gary Seath who came on board to help more on the operational side. He worked together with Stuart and me to get the first operational clients up and functioning. Gary exited our business after only a few years, but then went on to become a reward and recognition specialist and top consultant for Ernst & Young in Africa. Gary and I are still great mates and we still develop ideas and concepts together. He has a great passion for youth development and so do I, and so our paths often cross again and again. I am tremendously endeared to him for getting the operational side of our business up and growing.

There have been other influencers in our technology, and I have much to thank for our association with the mobile telecommunications industry and our clients in that space that were also new industries when they started years ago. They were the likes of Vodaphone in South Africa, and Vodacom was one of our very first technology and telecommunications clients. They obviously pushed us hard in terms of delivering unique solutions for them, and as a result we then also got to work for some of the major brands in the handset and mobile phone space, giants such as Nokia, Samsung, Huawei and Motorola. Those global businesses, that had very fast paced consumer goods in the tech space, also had their own tech specialists internally that had certain high demands and high expectations around the development. They pushed us competitively for more added value from our solutions, and these were the tools that sharpened us, focused us and kept us going. They kept us commercially relevant and helped grow our business substantially. These companies are also reinventing themselves and we have many of those relationships that still stand.

Again, I have a huge amount of gratitude for being able to work with such monster global companies. They really have helped shape us and build character into our technology, with the robustness and security level components needed when you work for German companies like Mercedes Benz and BMW. Their compliance around data integrity and that kind of thing are always top of mind and meeting those specifications at a global level has often not been easy, but it has pushed us to develop an understanding of what it takes to compete at a global digital secure level. We had to ensure our systems could not be hacked or passwords stolen and that there were no fraudulent activities.

There are many stories that Stuart can tell, on a much more detailed level, of how we grew and developed though sometimes very adverse situations. Understanding risk and what we needed to build into our technology to develop integrity around data security, areas of database information storage, backup support and fail-safe systems sharpened us and pushed us to the level of competence where we are today. That growth curve is always on, it's always steep, it's always demanding on-going learning and I think that is why I love the tech space so much. There's not a moment that you can say it's going to be the same next month as it was this month. One must always be on their toes innovating and I love it!

Thirty-Six

Anecdotes from Colleagues

"May there be many moments that make your life so sweet. Oh, but more than memories." - Mark Harris

by Huw Tuckett

I REMEMBER MY FIRST interview for Uwin Iwin, with Dave and Gail. I remember it was an interesting interview, Dave and I seemed to click immediately and liked each other from day one. Gail was a little bit more reserved as I remember. If I can recall, she was a little bit dubious because I only had inbound travel experience as opposed to outbound. But Dave did his normal maverick thing, and in the middle of the interview said "No, I think we should go ahead with this", which put Gail in a bit of a compromising position! Dave always did that, and still does that in fact. He wears his heart on his sleeve and regardless of what may come, is completely honest. That's a trait that I have always appreciated in him.

· · · · ● · ● · · · ·

I joined Uwin Iwin in 2003, towards the end of the year, and it was early days in the building in Rivonia. I have quite a few memories from that time, mainly of the people, Marlene and Gail, Judy was there also, busy with the Ford Academy. There was the craziness of the Vodacom travel accounts, they were by far our biggest client at that stage and had big expensive trips overseas. In the travel department, Elaine and Tanya were key people in the organisation at that stage. From a merchandise perspective, it was really the Ford Academy, and I remember Mathabo Power Tools used to send through loads and loads of vouchers for us to capture. The rewards were mostly Game, Dions and Pick n Pay vouchers if I can remember correctly and Marlene and Fikile used to count endless vouchers in the safe. There were tons of vouchers that we used to dispatch on a weekly basis; that was the reward of choice. We also had Barbara upstairs with Xenia Travel so that was another element of the business. They were good times, business was stable, business was good, and we were on the up.

Stuart was only working part time then if I remember, he was possibly even a subcontractor and I don't remember what version of NetUwin we were on then, but it was a very early version. Stuart used to pop in once or twice a week for a couple of hours just to see what he could do, so it was very low key. That continued for several years, and then we got quite successful on the online side of the business. We got into the mobile phone side a bit more, and I remember we picked up a big client, I think it was Cell C, and we started to do more and more for them. That was possibly even when we did the first debit card, the "Sell it, Coin it, Charge it" account. Roughly at the same time we also had Motorola as a client, so those were fairly big incentives that were kicking off and we had to upskill and get more people on board quite rapidly as I remember, and that prompted the move to bigger premises.

• • • •●•●• • ●

I was at Uwin Iwin for 12 years and I had some major life events happen while I was there, many of them very similar to Dave. We both went through the adoption process of our children, so we had something in common there. The other unfortunate thing was that we both lost our fathers in that time we worked together. David lost his dad first, and that was very poignant because Peter had been a major part of the business. He had always been there in the background, had always been the rock, the financial mainstay as it were of the business, just quietly providing that rudder and direction and guidance of what we should be doing. To a large extent my father was a huge rock in my life as well, so when we both lost our fathers, that brought myself and David very much closer together. It was very tough for both of us to handle, we both struggled with it immensely and it was a very difficult time personally in our lives. We were able to offer each other support and guidance and David was fantastic during my father's struggle.

We also had joyous times as well - the adoption of our children. Watching David go through the process, it was hugely enjoyable to see him grow as an instant dad. It was very similar to the way that I had as well because all of a sudden, we had these children, well not thrust upon us but it wasn't a lifestyle that we were used to! We had to adapt our lifestyles quite rapidly accordingly to suddenly having children in our lives, and we learned so much about ourselves individually as well. So that was a great time and we often used to share moments about what it was like to raise and rear children, and the frustrations that we used to have. As for the other life events, we also had the joy of birthdays – David had a fantastic 40th where we went to Mauritius, and he very kindly invited me and my family along. It was a truly wonderful experience. I had a fantastic 40th birthday party locally that everybody came to so there were some major events that happened during my time at Uwin Iwin.

. . . ●. ● . . .

I only ever saw David lose his temper three or four times in the twelve years that we worked together. I'll never forget one such occasion – we had an accountant who took it upon himself to borrow some of the company's money to fund some motor vehicle purchases, this was a young gentleman by the name of Sipho. We were alerted to the fact that some money had been diverted, did our research and investigation and eventually we found out and got the truth from him. David was so angry he made Sipho sit in his office. Sipho wasn't allowed to go anywhere or do anything and he wasn't even allowed to go into the bathroom until he told David what he had done with the money and how he had done it. David wasn't prepared to let him go until he had the full truth. I think David still went out for lunch and left Sipho sitting in his office, having told him that he better not move!

. . . ●. ● . . .

I think one of the most valuable lessons that I've ever learnt from David has been to contemplate and not to react quickly to certain situations. David taught me to stop, think about it, sleep on it, deliberate and look at the situation from different angles before responding, which is a very valuable skill and something that I have taken forward with me in my career. On numerous occasions we would have crisis situations, maybe even a complaint email from a client or a staff situation, but that calmness and that ability to not react now, but rather think about it first was a skill I really appreciate learning.

• • • • ● • ● • • •

Over the years I've seen David change in regard to his levels of impatience or his ability to increase his patience level. When I first met him, he used to be very impatient, and got very irritated with things – if he wanted it now, he wanted it done yesterday and of course that always led to amusing consequences especially relating to travel and traffic. If there was something in the way, very often David would steamroller it or push around it to get it done. This is yet another admirable quality that he has in that go-getter attitude, which I certainly didn't have, and I think that's why we complemented each other so well. I tend to sit back and watch, whereas David was very much a pathfinder and pushed through.

Sometimes there were some unrealistic expectations about how quickly things were supposed to happen. Speed has always been an element of the business which I think has trickled down from the top. David has been very good in communicating this, making sure that things could be done quickly, and should be done quickly. His philosophy was why allow bureaucracy to get in the way? Get it done and get it done now. As I say, this did lead to some amusing consequences especially at airports, restaurants, queues, and the list goes on...

• • • • ● • ● • • •

I recall one rather amusing incident. Dave and I used to travel quite a bit and he was always off in the world somewhere, so there was invariably a daily Skype call or at least a call every second day when we were travelling, just to check in and see how things were going. David was on a trip in Abu Dhabi, I don't know if it was a fam trip or a business trip or a SITE trip, but he was in a very posh hotel in Abu Dhabi somewhere. He skyped me from his glorious hotel room, then showed me with his computer what the room and the view looked like. Then he put the computer back down on the desk and continued to talk about business. He promptly took off his pants as he was getting changed, so there we were having this Skype call, with David walking around in his underwear, up and down the room with me trying very hard not to look and just remain focused on the conversation. After about ten minutes I recall him saying "Is the camera still on?" After a small hesitation I said "Yes" and he said "Oh. Sorry about that" and we both laughed.

Thirty-Seven

Property Investment and Move to New Offices in Kyalami

"In investing, what is comfortable is rarely profitable." - Robert Arnott

AFTER WE HAD RECOVERED from the initial separation from my previous partners, we had spent a couple of years getting back onto a growth path, paying back the debt that I had and getting a little bit of extra cash to invest. We moved and rented new offices at the bottom of Rivonia Road as I mentioned before. It was a nice self-contained unit of approximately four hundred square meters, with an upstairs and downstairs space of two hundred meters each. It had a little area outside where we could have lunches and things like that, and it was lovely. It then came up for sale on an auction, and my dad and I had a price in mind that we were prepared to take a punt on this property as we were very happy with it. Anyway, the auction came and went and we managed to secure a bid that was accepted, it was a little bit higher than we originally thought, but we could manage and that was our first property investment. I did that as an individual, the company paid me rent and I was able to pay the bond off. We were tenants and landlords. Of course it was a great investment because we would have had to pay rent anyway, and instead we were paying off a bond which we were able to do pretty quickly. It wasn't a huge number and we could manage it, and in the three or four years that we were there we paid off the investment. The business flourished and then we outgrew the property.

We needed more than four hundred square meters, because eventually we were jammed in like a bunch of sardines into this space. We needed to go and find a new property and the hunt was on for a new home for Uwin Iwin.

I decided I could do one of two things, find a new tenant for the existing building and go off and buy something else, or sell it. I decided to do the latter. I found a very good real estate broker who quickly got a couple of offers and I almost doubled my money in the three to four years on that investment. It turned out to be a phenomenal investment and it taught me a great deal about property and how you could actually make some real money out of property, sometimes much faster than you could make it out of operational turnover. I took my money and my wife and I then embarked on renovating and building and restoring our residential property, which was another very exciting thing that we did as a couple, and we now have a magnificent home that we are very, very proud of. We are extremely blessed to live in it with our children. Buying and selling that Rivonia property was one of those things that helped leverage and step us up into a property portfolio. It was an ideal situation to be in because we could live in a part of our investment, and then earn income from other property investments.

• • • • • • • • • •

The point of telling the story is if you can, as you're growing your entrepreneurial business, also look to build other assets other than just your business. My dad was always a keen proponent of making sure as an entrepreneur that you are also building a proper pension fund for yourself. You cannot have every single asset tied into one business, you've got to be investing in retirement annuities on a regular basis, making sure you have your life insurance and health plans and so on. That's one dynamic, but if one could then look to invest some of your surplus income or part of your salary into property, that's also a good idea as well as your own business. That way you are building assets as you go and not only when you ultimately sell off, or whatever your exit strategy might be to the next level of your business journey.

· · · · ●·●· · · ·

The other part of this story is an emotional one in a way. I had engaged with Arnd Herrmann to come out from Europe. We had originally met when he worked for a client of ours then we became quite good friends, and he was keen to help me find new premises. These we found rather close to where he was living in fact, in an office park very close to or rather across the road from the housing estate in which he had purchased a house. That's when we moved to Kyalami. It was an enormous property that had stood vacant for many years, it was a shell of a building, and we approached the landlord on the basis of "Hey, we'll go in there, we'll take the whole thing – we don't need the whole thing but you know, give us a really sexy lease and we'll fill it eventually!"

Wow, Arnie did fill it with many people, and it cost us plenty of money along the way! It was rather plush and lavish, and it had a spectacular view over the grand prix circuit of Kyalami racetrack. There was a beautiful view across the valley, looking towards Sandton with Johannesburg right in the background, a fabulous skyline view. I had a big corner office on the third floor and this was also very plush, I really indulged myself. Thinking back I was overly indulgent in this new property and my ego was fuelled, rather than thinking about some wise business decisions. I think that's part of the learning process for any young man in business and looking back it was probably a big mistake but nonetheless very exciting. We moved to this new property and started another phase of the journey and that's really the Arnie story where I appointed him as managing director of the business. We structured things differently and the idea was that I could get out of day to day operations and work more on the business and not IN the business.

· · · ● · ● · ● · · ·

We were also looking at starting a family. My wife and I had decided to adopt children because we couldn't have children of our own, despite having tried many of the fertility treatments that were available in those years. We had failed a few times on that, so God prompted us to go the adoption route to build a family, and I certainly then took plenty of time out of the business to focus on that. When we had the joy of fetching our son Daniel, and getting to be parents, Arne was so excited about that as well that he just wanted to give me as much time and space as I needed. I was so grateful for that. In its own way that created its own set of problems but at the time it was wonderful. I could leave the office early, spend time with the kids and with Dorcas, spend days at home and really enjoy that very, very special and unique part of my life journey. I have no regrets about that, and I am very thankful that I had that opportunity. Unfortunately, we had to do some fancy footwork a few years later to get back on track and in the saddle to take the business on another turn, but that was a great time in our lives and a very exciting phase in the business journey.

Thirty-Eight

Arne's Story...

"Climbing to the top demands strength, whether it is to the top of Mount Everest or to the top of your career." - A. P. J. Abdul Kalam

By Arnd Herrmann

MY TIME AT UWIN IWIN – or why not climb a mountain without the leader.....

It was that time again! Every month some representative from this external company was expected to visit our offices at Siemens. At that time, the otherwise rather pathetic (sorry, guys!) Sales Representatives stretched their legs, went to the bathroom to freshen up and started to pace up and down the corridor, reminding me every time of the feeding times at the zoo (with all respect to my ex-colleagues; I might exaggerate slightly!) You could feel the (positive) tension rising in the office and as soon as the expected person had arrived and put a document up on the wall, which I later learned was called "Leaderboard", the noise level and blood pressure shot up.

It was an amazing sight and I started wondering what the secret recipe of this company was to generate this kind of reaction from the crowd.

It was not only during this monthly 'feeding time' where those guys from this external agency made a difference to our business life, no! The absolute highlight of each year was the Sales Conference, organised by the same company – the, and I don't say this lightly, THE talking point for the next few days, no, what am I saying, weeks! Everybody, and I mean this literally, everyone (me included) was jealous each year we were not allowed to attend, and excited if we (those that didn't have the privilege to be called 'sales representative') had the opportunity to be part of this event.

One day, I actually grabbed the young gentleman that had just fulfilled the monthly duty. I am reverting back to the 'feeding time' here, and while our Sales Reps were digesting the food, I asked him about this "You win I something" company and what they were all about. I then listened in amazement to the story of this organisation, how they had started, grown, added new services, and how they were now running incentive programs and events for Corporates. My heartbeat went up, and the thought crossed my mind how exciting it must be to work for a company like this where everything is about something positive: Rewards, Recognition, Motivation, Incentives. Little did I know that a few years later, I would do exactly this – join this awesome company!

The gentleman that had given me this exciting 'pep-talk', as I found out later, was none other than the founder of this great team, and I had just had my first encounter with Mr. David Sand. It was an informal conversation on the floor that was the start of an amazing and wonderful friendship. At the same time, it would lead into a similarly exciting and successful business relationship; the former to last forever, the latter unfortunately coming to a painful finish a few years later.

• • • •**•**•**•** • • •

I will never forget the evening in October 2004 – my wife Petra, and our two kids Kayleigh and Nicholas had just arrived at David and Dorcas's place to start our two-week holiday in our adopted home country, South Africa. During our welcome braai my friend gave me an update about his company, telling me that his business partner Gail Botha had decided to leave the team to start a family and another business. He was now looking for someone to join the team and help him grow the business, ideally to the stage of being an internationally acknowledged organisation.

With a friendly "this would be something for you, Arnie", David slapped me on my back. I am not sure if he knew back then what he was up for in the following years; I certainly didn't.... "No ways" was my initial thought, despite my interest in Uwin Iwin when I first met David a few years earlier. My resistance was not loudly proclaimed though! We had left South Africa for very good (actually very bad) reasons (crime, high interest rates and the lot) four years earlier. I worked at General Electric's Bank in Switzerland and had become the guy climbing the corporate career ladder in my dream company. I had always been a fan of Jack Welch, joining this great, but at the same time, rather medium sized enterprise.

The seed had been planted though. Many old friends showered us with their love during our vacation and we actually fell in love with South Africa all over again – but moving back? After having spent a few days in the Pilanesberg, I asked my precious wife how she felt about this crazy idea. She said, "On arrival it was 2/10, now I am on 5/10." This was her immediate response, to which I answered, "Well it's 12/10 from my side!"

I came back to Jo'burg over a weekend in November to talk about these details. David and I both spent hours talking about roles and responsibilities, company structure, expectations, objectives, aspirations, and we were singing from the same song sheet, like good friends and business entrepreneurs sometimes do.

But could Uwin Iwin afford me? Would I be able to adjust my financial expectations from a global Corporate to getting paid by a local SME? I still remember that I suggested for David and his Finance Manager to sit and do their calculations together in one room, while I would do some research about the money. I needed to maintain our lifestyle in another room. The idea was for each of us then to put a number on a piece of paper, pray about it, turn the paper around, and if the difference between those figures would be too high, we would call it quits. If it was 'in range'', we would negotiate, and in the highly unlikely event that the numbers were the same, God wanted us to go ahead with this idea, and so we began.

After two hours of intense Exceling, Googling and using calculators, we sat down in David's office again. In anticipation and with excitement we both were holding our piece of paper upside down. We then turned the documents around - our two numbers were out by only R500! Amazed and relieved, we hugged each other. We now knew that God was in this with us if He had guided us both to come to the same result.

I wondered why God would support this kind of crazy plan. Back at home, I prayed about this opportunity again and again. I felt that He was calling me back to South Africa, not only to help David grow the business, but also to relieve my friend from work responsibilities, allowing him to focus on the adoption process which I knew was so important for him and his wonderful wife, Dorcas. Allow me to jump forward in time briefly: I am so happy that those two wonderful friends can call two equally wonderful boys their children now, and I am excited to see those two boys, who are now young men, grow up!

· · · ● · ● · · · ·

It was 2005 now, and I had returned to South Africa to start a new chapter in my and my family's life. I was taking over the responsibility for marketing and merchandise at Uwin Iwin, while David stayed at the helm of the organisation. A gentleman from England, Huw Tuckett would remain in charge of the travel and events side of the business, and Elize was looking after the finances.

This was the start of a mostly amazing time. It was a rather 'interesting" start which was a bit of a culture shock to me and nothing I had expected. I remember my first management meeting vividly. It was my first week, I had only just started to get to know the people, the processes, the products, the customers, and I was told that I was expected to fire one of my team members since she was not performing in her role at all. Firing people in my first week? I thought this was all about motivation, recognition, and rewards, and the first thing I was asked to do is to get rid of someone, a person I had hardly been introduced to. I very kindly asked to please give me some time first to at least get to know this lady, find out why she wasn't performing and for me then to judge if a dismissal was indeed the last option. I was very delighted that my request was granted.

So off I went to meet and get to know my team better. There she was, the lady in question, who was a member of the marketing team. She was responsible for designing and developing the creative campaigns, and for sourcing the teasers and gifts that we would be using to get the relevant participants of our incentive programs excited about the upcoming trips.

The only challenge I figured out very quickly was that this woman had very limited (I am polite here) creativity in her DNA, which made it slightly difficult for her to fulfil her duty. The only thing she actually did was pass on the briefs from a client, and not an easy client I may mention here, an external agency. The agency would then come up with ideas and she would forward those ideas back to the client. So she was giving zero, but seriously zero value-add to our client.

Instead, as I figured out, she was very good in admin and had a passion for customer service. Get her on the phone to speak to a participant and she would take care of the inquiry in the most professional manner; ask her to monitor and report on incoming orders or outgoing deliveries, and you wouldn't find a single mistake. So to cut this story short, she didn't get fired. I transferred her into a new role, and she really hated me for this initially; but she grew amazingly in her new responsibility. She was eventually promoted and became one of my key people in Merchandise Rewards. She unfortunately left the company years later due to relocation to Cape Town, but what an asset she had become!

This was one of many stories of people joining (and leaving) the team during those four years I had the privilege to be part of Uwin Iwin, some other highlights in short:

We had a lady that told us that the main reason for her applying for this role was the proximity of the office to her home. David and I (and she herself, realising what she had said) almost fell off our chairs! We still took her on board and she became a rather successful Business Development Manager.

· · · ●· ● · ·

I brought a new Team Leader on board for our Call Centre, and after a while our data usage went up sky-high, and the productivity of our team went down significantly – until I found out that this gentleman was sourcing and distributing funny videos on the Internet in the hundreds every week, using our entire bandwidth and, of course, entertaining the team but keeping them away from work while watching all those clips!

· · · · ●· ● · · ·

One day we had a rather critical meeting with one of our biggest clients, a global Telecom company, at their headquarters in Midrand. By that time, David had given me the opportunity to take over the overall responsibility of the company and I was now the Managing Director. In this new role I was expected to attend these meetings, together with Uwin Iwin's Account Manageress Jill, our merchandise representative Pam, and two other members of the team. Our counterpart was a Vice President, known to be very critical, abrupt, strict, and not an easy person to deal with. I had managed to build a rather good relationship with him over time. Anyway, Pam and I entered the meeting room a few minutes after the official start of the meeting, this due only to their reception taking forever to check us in. Not unexpectedly, this gentleman had started the meeting already. As we entered, he briefly looked at us, stopped mid-sentence and then spoke into his dictaphone, "For the record, Arne Herrmann and Pam Williams from Uwin Iwin have now finally joined the meeting five minutes after nine." I couldn't believe my ears! Pam blushed, her blood pressure must have doubled, and the atmosphere in the room changed from cool to ice-cold. I really had to bite my tongue not to respond to this. It was insulting, and this from someone I did not only respect but thought I had a good relationship with.

Upset, and embarrassed I took my seat, took out my notepad, breathed in deeply to relax and looked to our host to enter the discussion – and had to laugh inwardly since the VP looked at me with a big grin, and winked at me making it clear that he was just fooling around with me and all of us! I relaxed, while poor Pam was hectically taking notes, jotting down all the sometimes rather silly requests.

As the saying goes, you always meet again. Months later, we had a follow-up meeting. It was the Vice President, another high up member of the board, Jill, and I in his office. This time he was more relaxed, and we were talking about the previous activities and successful engagements. Then he suddenly looked at his watch and told us that he had to leave the meeting early due to some other commitments. This resulted in me taking out my mobile phone, pretending it was a dictaphone and stating loud and clearly, "For the record, Michael A. from V. is leaving a meeting that was set up from 13H00 until 14H00, 15 minutes prior to the scheduled finish time." He, the other board member and I had the laugh of our life. Poor Jill, not knowing about the background, must have died a thousand deaths, thinking that I had just ruined the relationship with our top client. Jill, if you read this story – please forgive me!

Thirty-Nine

Acquisition Target Explained

"The desire for knowledge, like the thirst of riches, increases ever with the acquisition of it." - Laurence Sterne

IT WAS NOW 2008 and the business had been growing at a clip. I had gone through the phase of being a daddy and just kind of chairman of the business, and Arnie was running it as a managing director. I was also very much involved as a global leader and I was deeply involved in the SITE community around the world. I was attending global conferences, bringing back the latest and greatest trends and tech development and so on from all over the world. I was bringing them back home to South Africa, re-engineering them for our own purposes and really being a bit of a figurehead. I made friends with so many people around the world and our business became quite interesting for those bigger companies. What we did and how we did it, and the stories that I told about our businesses made it a sexy target for an acquisition by an international company.

I was quite keen on becoming part of a global community, and one of the ways I thought I could do this was to use the Uwin Iwin South Africa business as a leverage or stepping stone into a global career. I didn't really want to go back into running the South African business; I now wanted to look for the next horizon. This came in the form of an international Swiss business that wished to acquire us or showed an interest to acquire us. I fostered that idea. We started talking, and the founder and CEO of that business and I started getting closer together. They saw a piece of their puzzle and their vision being fulfilled and I could fill a small part of that bigger vision they had for their business.

Two executives came out from Switzerland and visited our fancy offices in Kyalami. They spent some time, stayed at my home and really got to see South Africa. I remember one of the nice things we organised was a helicopter flip from the Kyalami helicopter pad. We rolled out of our offices in my big Mercedes Benz that I had spoiled myself with, and we drove to the helicopter pad and got into the helicopter. They were mightily impressed; they were quite cool guys as well who liked the good life. We took off and we flew over our office park, took a few pictures then did an aerial spin over Jo'burg. We showed them all the hotspots, flew over Soweto and the football stadium that was being built for the World Cup to come and it was very exciting.

We concluded that with quite a deep dive into how our business worked, and it was amazing talking to guys that were well skilled in the art of mergers and acquisitions. I was very wet behind the ears when it came to that. I had started reading some books and had realised that there was so much that I knew that I didn't know! So, we entered this cautiously and it was a big number that was put on the table, and I was very excited about this.

One of the things that really enticed me was a career where I would be put on an international board to head the development of the global business, basically by taking the Uwin Iwin model in South Africa and applying it to their multiple business units around the world. I think at that stage they were in something like twenty-odd countries around the world, and I was to implement the Uwin Iwin success that we had in one country, in twenty, effectively doing a multiple of twenty times the Uwin Iwin South Africa business. That was so exciting and very enticing, and I got romanced into this process.

Arnie was very unsure of this and he, coming from a big corporate background, didn't want to go from being in an entrepreneurial small business back into a big corporate. I on the other hand had always been a little entrepreneur desiring to be a big guy, a big fish ultimately in a big pond. So we structured a deal where an agreement was signed, pending due diligence. I would then get involved in the international board, they gave me a fancy title, I would have quarterly board meetings all over the world from Toronto to Switzerland to Asia, and all over the place. It really was the start of this sort of jet set global business career, or so I thought.

There were a lot of stressful things happening in the world at that time, including the global financial crisis that started with the collapse of the junk bond market in the US, and then the subsequent collapse of the banking industry in New York. That rippled on to Europe and so on, creating a global financial crisis that then saw our customers losing huge traction, not having the money to spend with us ultimately. We ended up being at the short end of the corporate austerity measures, where they cut absolutely all spending on incentives and incentive travel. Our business tanked and it was in the middle of this acquisition or sales process that this happened.

It was very ugly, and one thing I knew, deep in my heart, was that in that environment that we were experiencing, there was absolutely no way that I would ever be able to make or get our business to do a U-turn and meet all of the profit guarantees that were, or would be pencilled into a final sale agreement. It would just not turn around that quickly. I had the balls to go to the international board and tell them this was not working, and it couldn't possibly work this way. I needed to pull out of this deal and go back home to Johannesburg with my tail between my legs and fix my business. Then if we were all still interested, we could talk later once the financial crisis had run its course and we had recovered.

That unfortunately upset the international company; I think they fully understood the rationale, but I don't think they had ever had somebody do a U-turn on an acquisition deal before.

To save face for them and for us, I then sold them our Cape Town business, or rather, 50% of our Cape Town business. That we then carved out and rebranded as a South African destination management company that they then had a large stake in. A couple of years later I sold my 50% outright to them so that they had 100% ownership of that Cape Town business. They subsequently went on to continue to grow and operate under their global brand name in South Africa, and I am glad that was a success.

Having gone through that, being an acquisition target taught me a huge amount of things. None other was more important than to pay attention to what your balance sheet looked like, and what your loan accounts were looking like, in short the forensic due diligence process that we went through as a business with a local company, and the due diligence arm of a French global audit firm called Mazars. It was an eye-opening process and I can really recommend that as a key learning part of an entrepreneur's journey. When you decide to sell a business, one needs to know what to do to get the due diligence done smoothly, and in a way that adds value to your sale price. There's a whole art and science in that, and obviously the key of that is integrity around your accounting and your processes. That we didn't have a problem with, but we were certainly naïve in some aspects of how we structured our balance sheet. It wasn't so much for the sake of enhancing our balance sheet value; that was never a prime focus for us, but it's an important part of an exit or an acquisition strategy or when acquiring a new business. It was an invaluable learning process for me.

I'm pleased to say that at a global level, we are still very much respectful of each other as two parties in this space. We've managed to keep our relationships intact for which I am very grateful. I learnt a huge amount through that process, but I am also grateful in another way that the circumstances allowed me to keep pushing on with my own journey. Sometimes I am amazed to think I was protected at so many points in my business journey from being involved with partners. I was protected from an acquisition and still came out the other side with something that I can call my own. The business is still growing, and for us looking into the future, there's still the opportunity to do acquisition growth ourselves. We could implement some of the learnings that we have got from being an acquisition target, going through the proper due diligence processes, knowing what to look for and how to finesse certain deals or how not to mess them up.

The other aspect of it is obviously, as a business, we are always now very attentive to making sure that our balance sheet processes are well defined. They are absolutely bullet proof in terms of the standard or generally accepted accounting principles, taxation issues and risk management things that are all very important to the value of a business, and of course to the customer contracts, all of those good things that secure and define an ongoing business concern that is of value.

Forty

Consolidation, Move to Bryanston and the Oval Office

"Life's challenges are not supposed to paralyze you, they're supposed to help you discover who you are." - Bernice Johnson Reagon

THE GLOBAL FINANCIAL CRISIS produced yet another devastating effect on our business. Turnover dropped by almost 70% in that single year. We had a cash flow crisis of massive proportions given our large staff complement expensive officers and expensive tech and R&D division. Again I was at the place where I was humbled by circumstances I needed to get stuck back in the middle of a crisis. This crisis was yet another near death experience for Uwin Iwin. The odds looked incredibly stacked against us surviving for the first time ever. It was almost impossible to find new clients and generate success from sales and new customer acquisition. There was only one way to possibly give us a chance and that was to downsize the business to an affordable level. So we embarked upon a corporate restructuring where we had to say farewell to almost 50% of our team that amounted to 30 people who he loved and cared for. We also had to get rid of all unnecessary expenses and one of those big expenses was quite a hefty rental contract for our officers. I instructed the team to cancel our lease and find much smaller premises. We also had a rather awkward situation with the receiver of revenue because we were unable to pay staff and the retrenchment packages and then pay the tax man. We were in a real mess and I really didn't see a way through.

One of the long term relationships that we had formed was with Sean Sim, our legal counsel. I set up a meeting to go and see Sean together with Huw, who had at that stage become the replacement managing director Arnd Herman who had exited the business. Before going to the meeting Huw and I stood on the balcony of Arnie's old office, He was chain smoking due to all of the stress and I was trying to hold it together and put on a brave face. But as I was leaning over the balcony I had this very dark thought that I was worth more dead to the business than alive. My life insurance cover at that stage, if paid out would have been almost exactly what was required to get us out of the hole. I said to Huw, "Well maybe it's just better if I jump." He quickly got me inside and ready for the meeting. After an hour of mopping and moaning and telling our sad story to Sean he said guys listen I don't have any more time for this nonsense what you need to do is the following, set up a meeting with the SARS and negotiate a way forward and then get back to work and save this business you can do it. We really wanted advice on how to shut the business down and save face he was having none of it.

Our trip to SARS was a nightmare, I hadn't slept for about a week. I remember heading to the SARS office in Sunninghill sitting down in a rather dingy little office and being faced by a rather vicious tax officer. But we managed to negotiate the six month stay of execution and were told in no uncertain terms, if we failed to make the payments we could be arrested. Thank God we were able to make a plan and make the payments.

The time came for us to move. We packed our stuff, I left on a trip I hadn't even seen the new officers and arrived back in South Africa to a new office setup which I really didn't like at first but came to love. The new office again gave us that iconic place of a new birth and the remaining team were happy to shoulder the load and get the job done in terms of managing clients and getting new opportunities on the table. Huw was a tremendous managing director; he was pragmatic, prudent, practical and had a great rapport with staff and clients. I was so over my ego that I didn't even want an office. I was quite happy to have a small place to work and rather let the rest of the team take up the best spots in the office. I felt beaten, defeated and certainly humbled. Just a few months earlier I had millions of Rand on the table for the sale of my business into a global business and now my wings were clipped, my dreams shattered and the value of the business on paper was almost zero. I really had to dig deep to put on a bright face to refocus and create a new dream.

One of the amazing things that I had learned being part of this international board was the concept of a painted picture which really was a strategy document that crystallized a very clear picture of where the business needed to go. So I gathered the team and said let's create our very own painted picture of the future and what this business should look like in a three-year term. My wife and I had gone into partnership with another couple that we had met and had purchased a beautiful beach property in Princess Grant golf estate on the Kwa Zulu Natal North Coast. The team joined me down at the house we fitted into the house and some rooms at the lodge. It was a fantastic exercise that recalibrated the business and defined and prioritized the key parts of the business plan we need to attack and get right. It really energized me and the team but especially me I was able to again see a path and the goal that I needed to run up.

Implementing and executing on the plan was so exciting, each part of the team worked highly efficiently and diligently towards that goal without much requirement for motivating and leading from me. Huw was really the champion. It seemed to spring into place the moment we got back, lots of prayer, many new miracles, huge amounts of hard work and dedication and we were quickly on the rebound.

The Oval office Park in Bryanston was our new home and we flourished.

Forty-One

My Life, My Wife, My Driving Force

"Happy is the man who finds a true friend, and far happier is he who finds that true friend in his wife." – Franz Schubert

THIS IS A CHAPTER that I want to dedicate to my wife, a massive driving force in my life. My wife's name is Dorcas Margaret Sand, her maiden name was Lunn . She is the middle child in a family with an older brother Glen, and a younger brother Adrian. They were born in Zambia, Northern Rhodesia at the time, in Lusaka. Her father was always in colonial administrative roles, and her mother didn't work, not until later years. They grew up in beautiful parts of Northern Rhodesia, and then eventually moved to Southern Rhodesia, known today as Zimbabwe. Dorcas always went to good schools. Her relationship with her brothers was good - she always describes them as great fun, albeit mischievous. Her brothers were typical boys and I think she bore the brunt of some of their antics.

But even from a very, very young age, Dorcas was a person who always strove to live a life that was righteous or right. She was not a naughty girl, she never has been a naughty girl, and she always tries to be a moral upstanding citizen. Not only that, from a very early age she had a relationship with God. Dorcas tells me about how she used to write prayers and poems to the Lord. She used to pray to the Lord often, and as a young girl she always prayed that she would have a beautiful wedding someday and that she would meet her Prince Charming. She also prayed that she would not have many boyfriends, but she would meet the right man to fall in love with, and love for the rest of her life. This is part of her love story, and my love story – in that God did connect us, two very, very different people, and He has kept us together, and hopefully will keep us together for eternity.

· · ● · ● · ● · ● · · ·

Dorcas's life in Zimbabwe was traumatised by the Rhodesian bush war. Her father was obviously involved in quasi-government or regional administration, in the town council. He was the mayor or the deputy mayor of a town called Chinoyi, after the fall of the Ian Smith government. Her father then had the task of training and developing the town's first black mayor who funnily enough was an albino guy, a black man with a pale skin discoloration. I'm sure if he was still alive, Ian would be able to tell many funny and interesting stories about that time of his life!

Prior to that, her elder brother Glen was shipped off to schooling in the UK to get a good education there, and possibly to avoid being drafted into the military. Glen finished his schooling in the UK and as I understand it, returned to Zimbabwe. Much to his parents' horror, Glen enlisted in the military, not only as a regular troop but his desire was to join the Rhodesian Selous Scouts which is an exclusive, high profile unit that was deeply involved in forward reconnaissance and high contact military action – a group like the British SS. The Selous Scouts were famous around the world for their courage and battle hardiness.

Anyway, with that came the incredible stress and tension of an older brother being involved in that kind of action and a father that was called up on a bi-weekly basis to do civilian military duty. There was a war raging, a terrorist war, a war of freedom fighting where previously disenfranchised black members were fighting for the right to vote and to govern. That war ended with the Smith administration agreeing to grant the franchise to all citizens including black citizens of Rhodesia. An election was held and a new government came into power.

· · · · ·•·•·•· · · ·

The Lunn family then decided that it was time to relocate. They relocated or immigrated to South Africa and left Zimbabwe behind. Dorcas often talks about the trauma of that, a convoy of cars leaving Harare in the early morning hours, shotgun out the window of the car. They were escorted by military escorts to the South African border. They then crossed the border into this new country, and drove all the way down to Grahamstown, where her father had got a job as an administrator of the university. They moved from a warm, beautiful climate to a climate in the Eastern Cape that was anything but warm and friendly – you could have many seasons in one day, and the winter temperatures got very cold, below freezing even. Dorcas absolutely hated it and her mother hated it too I think and suffered a bit of depression at that time. Glen the elder brother had left the military and went to Johannesburg, so there was a split in the family. Her younger brother Adrian was still at school, so they both finished their schooling in South Africa. Dorcas had to learn the South African second language, Afrikaans, and complete her matric year at Victoria Girls High in Grahamstown. It was a very traumatic time, tough time from many aspects indeed.

Dorcas and I met briefly at Rhodes University, but because she was a good girl as I described earlier, she was flying academically. She also was and still is a very beautiful woman, and she got involved in modelling. She was the top model for an outfit in the Eastern Cape and she always had the privilege of wearing the wedding gown creative, or the most creative piece on the runway at the time. So she was academic and beautiful. She IS academic and beautiful, and she is incredibly hard working. Even at university she was working two or three jobs to help earn an income and pocket money for herself. She was living at home and working hard too, when I was on campus living in residence, fully funded by my parents. I was partying like crazy, and failing all my academics or scraping through, making my journey just that much more difficult, even though I certainly had plenty of fun in the process. So we met only very briefly at university, and again once we had both graduated. We started our careers, and Dorcas joined Woolworths after studying an honours or BA course in English linguistics. She joined Woolworths as a management trainee, and got promoted very quickly, thus began her first couple of years at Woolworths.

• • • • • • • • • •

I had been unemployed for about six months, and then I found a job with Anglo American, as a trainee human resource guy. Probably a year or two later, we met at several post-Rhodes University parties in Johannesburg, where the clan gathered to reminisce about old times at university and to party up a storm. We saw each other at a party at the Hard Knock Residence near Corlett Drive, Johannesburg, where many of the old Rhodes guys that were in the drinking clubs and ex-Winchester House guys that I knew very well, were living. When I saw her, she told me that she was soon going with Helen, a friend of hers, to Europe as an overseas experience. I was delighted to meet up with her again and was really a bit star-struck by her and her beauty, but disappointed that she was going to be heading off into the world and I wouldn't really be able to build a relationship with her.

Anyway, before she left we saw each other a few times. I was training at the new health fad gym in Johannesburg which was the Sandton Health and Racquet Club, with the major Johannesburg yuppies and their Porsches and Ferraris. I was driving a BMW 3 series and I thought I was cool. Dorcas and her buddy Helen also trained a couple of times there and we'd bump into each other there, so she became quite visible on my radar. Then she and Helen did go on their overseas experience, it was almost a year and a half or two years of travelling, and I carried on my career. During that time, I got engaged to a lady that I'd met at the Health and Racquet Club, her name was Janine, and Dorcas had gotten engaged overseas to an Australian guy.

Dorcas returned from somewhere, Thailand I think, and was very ill with Salmonella. She had picked up this food carried bug that was quite dangerous, and so that had put an end to her travels. She had to come back home, clean up her salmonella, get healthy again, and then she started her career again with Woolworths. It wasn't long after her return that she and I bumped into each other at a Woolworths store in Rivonia near to where I lived. She was working there and had just recently opened that store. I remember seeing her, she saw me at the same time and it was quite a shock encounter in one way. We greeted each other and we were nice and pleasant to each other. I said, "Oh so you're back, and how are you?" and she said "Yes, I'm back and I'm engaged." That was a bit of a bombshell to me, but I was also engaged, and I put my own bombshell on the table and said, "Yeah, I'm also engaged!" I think there was a measure of disappointment in both of our voices after that, and we passed a few more pleasantries before saying goodbye. I turned around and walked out of the store with my groceries, and she carried on managing the store and life went on.

• • • • • • • • • •

Maybe six months later, we bumped into each other again at a pub. It was quite interesting because I had been partying like crazy. I had broken off my engagement about four months previously. The reason I broke off my relationship with Janine was because it wasn't going well, I had really decided that she wasn't the one for me and I had to be honest with myself and with her. The wedding date had been set and the invitations had gone out, so it was quite traumatic for her and for me. Obviously, it took courage to be completely honest, but I had mustered this and broken it off. So four months later I met up with Dorcas again, but between this and breaking off my relationship to be married to Janine, I had gone off the rails a little bit. I had been drinking heavily, I was partying big time, I was dating girls left, right and centre because I was now back on the market as it were, single. I had friends that were very keen to convince me that this single life of non-committal philandering was the way to go, and it was all a bit crazy.

I got to the point, before the evening when I met Dorcas again that I had decided enough was enough. I was not going out for another party. I had told all my mates I was not going out because I had some work to do on my home. I had invented this excuse but then decided to paint my bathroom and spruce it up. I had bought this beautiful duplex townhouse in Sunninghill and I was in the process of making it my own, putting my own personal signature on this home, decorating it. I started painting out this bathroom – and it was a great distraction, and I had purpose. I was painting away, and just enjoying my own company, and the peace and quiet of being at home. I got to about 10.30 on Friday night and I had completed painting my bathroom. I took a shower in another bathroom, cleaned myself up and went upstairs.

I was about to get into bed when I started wondering what all my buddies were doing, and where they were. The temptation to go out and hook up with them was very strong. As this was the day before cell phones and WhatsApp and SMSs, I didn't quite know where they were and I guessed that they would be at a pub in Rosebank at about that time, so I headed off to this pub called Hoods. Hoods was a pumping, trendy, hook-up place of note, and a very social, Jo'burg Friday night drinks party place. As I was arriving, Dorcas and her friend Helen were leaving. The pub was so jam-packed you had to kind of squeeze your way in and squeeze your way out, and we were standing body to body almost in the entrance passageway to the pub. We greeted each other briefly amongst the din of the busy pub. Then the two of them left and I continued to go in. Dorcas and her friend got to the carpark then Dorcas said to Helen something like, "I need to go back in, he's the one for me" and Helen reacted with shock. Anyway, they did come back in and we spent some time together.

****

The next day I got a call from Dorcas inviting me to a braai, and I told her arrogantly that I no longer did braais and she was quite annoyed by that. Anyway, Helen then phoned me a week or so later to invite me to attend an evening meal at another party venue called the Rattlesnake Roadside Diner, which was an amazing place for great entertainment, great music and great food. After clarifying that it was Dorcas who had extended the invitation, I said I would be there. That evening was a challenging one for me because Dorcas spent the whole evening telling me, in front of all these people, what an idiot I was, how arrogant I was and that I really needed to be a little less arrogant. I deserved most of it but it was a bit of a shock! I didn't expect it to be honest, but everything that she said rang true – I was arrogant, I was obnoxious, I was on a path of total destruction and self-indulgence and I wasn't really that nice a person to be around, to be honest. I had taken on this young up and coming, professional Johannesburg win at all costs, self-centred materialistic value set. I went home that night and really pondered all these things that she had said, and I was troubled with myself.

But still I wanted to see her again; something powerful was attracting me to her. It was her goodness, and I saw her as this almost unattainable model of a woman, a woman of great integrity, of great beauty, courage and intelligence. I realised this was the woman that I wanted to marry, and I realised it quickly – but I didn't know what I was going to do about it. A few more dates later, one night I was so troubled I was in tears, and she thought I was trying to break it off. I was just trying to articulate what I really thought of her, about how I loved her and how she inspired me to move towards something much better and I wasn't finding the words. The result of that conversation was that I then said to her that I really didn't want to break it off and I was making this huge choice in my life to move away from a certain direction towards another direction, and that I actually wanted to marry her.

I was invited on a trip to Austria, so Dorcas and I went there for a skiing holiday. Not long after we came back, I booked us into a lodge in northern Natal. We drove down to this beautiful lodge and I proposed to Dorcas. I asked her to marry me about six months after we had met again at Hoods and thank God she said yes. We were very excited, we set a wedding date and we had a very short engagement of around six months. We got married in August, after a very trying start to our wedding day as I have described earlier in the book.

• • • •●•●• • • •

I want to pay tribute to my wife because of her relationship with God from an early age, her decision to live a righteous life, to strive to be a woman of integrity, to live by her own moral code that always honoured God. She does her best, with an incredible work ethic, and lives a no-nonsense, straightforward, brutally honest life. Because that, and I only so many years later can write this because it's taken me so long to realise, is really what it is about, what attracted me to her. I must give so much credit to Dorcas for being the one who inspired me to want to have a relationship with God first of all. It was her inspiration in our early days that made me want to seek a different path, from a path of selfishness and self-destruction which I was definitely on, to have a life similar to hers. I wanted to follow her direction, to be a good citizen and a good person. To be less self-centred and less arrogant was a start to that.

Her relationship with God also started me on my journey for my own relationship with God. It inspired me to go to church with her and sit there and think about God and think about my relationship with God and hear a few sermons, and read a bible now and again and start to pray. Of course, my own testimony is that a business colleague of mine then got me much closer to the Lord and I have through many years given him, Eugene de Villiers, all or most of the credit for being the one that gave me the nudge towards the Lord. But actually, before Eugene de Villiers even thought about or was prompted to do anything with me, my wife was the one who was the original inspiration. Her example, not by her words, but by her deeds and rather by her life and the way she lived and honoured God, set me on a path that would eventually lead to having a relationship with the Lord Jesus. So, I need to give her so much credit for that.

The other reason I need to honour Dorcas is that my wife has always, as a career woman, made more than an equal contribution to our relationship and our financial wellbeing. She has worked for over thirty years for Woolworths, and she has gone up, and up, promoted from one job to the next job so that she is now a very senior person in operations regionally for Woolworths. Her operating or sales budget is in excess of two billion rand and the weight of that responsibility is massive. She manages in excess of 25 stores and store managers that report to her, and within her business unit there are probably in excess of 1000, probably 2000+ people that report into her business structure. So, she continues to be this incredible woman, a business leader and incredible business driver. Dorcas is hard-working, ethical and she draws a good monthly salary. She's been rewarded with share schemes, bonuses and performance bonuses through the years that have really carried us and enabled us to live in a wonderful home. Together we can afford the things that we afford, the holidays, and now with the children, being able to pay for their schooling, and all those nice little necessities that really make our life comfortable and joyful.

Dorcas is in the process of amassing a fair size pension. I didn't always understand this, but she doesn't spend money flippantly. She works hard for it and she knows the value of money. She'll walk into a store and look at all these beautiful new things. Of course her retail background is in fashion, she loves fashion, she studies it, she knows what the latest trends are, the latest colours, the latest fabrics, but she'll walk into a store and admire a brand new piece such as a jacket, or a beautiful blouse or something like that, and she will refrain from whipping out her credit card and purchasing it, even though she could afford it. She would rather wait a full season until the sales, and hopefully that item may be on sale. Very often, that item IS on sale, in her size, and she purchases it at about 50% of the price that it was on the peg the day it was launched to the consumers.

That's the kind of woman she is with her money, and she always puts the right decision forward and the right decision-making process forward. Dorcas thinks about what she does, she thinks about what she says. In everything she does, she asks herself the question, "Is this the right thing to do?"

Of course, she makes mistakes, but I'm talking about in general, and I have to honour her for that. I look at her, and she's always been that example to me, because I'm not that kind of guy. I'm a risk taker, I'm the guy that when I see it and I want it, I get it, and sometimes that has landed me in very tough financial circumstances because I have been irresponsible in the way I have handled my money. But I'm learning, I'm still learning from her and she has continued to keep her faith – she and I were baptised together, we committed our lives, we became born again together, we have run a church fellowship group in our home for over 20 years together. We have nurtured people, we have grown together, we have prayed together, and we continue to do that. We love each other, we've loved people, we've supported people, and she does that with a free heart and a commitment to the Lord and the Kingdom of God. She genuinely first seeks the Kingdom of God before she seeks the things that she needs in her life.

• • • ● • ● • • • •

As a mother, Dorcas is incredible. In the last eleven years since we've had children in our lives, wow, she has never taken any nonsense. She loves with all of her heart and everybody knows that. I love the joy that I see on her face when she spends time with our boys. They snuggle and they love and they care for each other. She has such joy in buying them little things and teaching them how to find things on sale, and she's been a spectacular choice for my life – thank you, God! We are so, so different. She's this filing cabinet of precision, of thoughtfulness, of order, of conservatism, of incredible good looks; I am a rain cloud of hope, of excitement, sometimes changing shapes as I come across the horizon, going from light to dark, thunder to lightning, to crash, to pour down the rain then sometimes I disappear. I am chaotic at times, I am a risk taker, I'm so different, and she has struggled through the years to nurture that difference and to fully understand it. All I can do is thank Dorcas for being so patient with me. I have struggled sometimes with the structure and the discipline and the rigidity of her personality, but it's been good for me.

Dorcas, my wife, my life, my driving force - I have learned so much from you, and I love you with all my heart. God knows your name – He loves you, Baby, and I love you too. Thank you for the joy you've brought to my life already, and for the many more beautiful years that we're still going to share. I pray to God that I live a long and happy life so that I can enjoy so much more with you – and most of all, thank you for being you.

Forty-Two

Kenya

"Everyone wants to live on top of the mountain, but all the happiness and growth occurs while you're climbing it." – Andy Rooney

2012 TO 2014 WERE interesting years as we started the Africa Growth Path for Uwin Iwin International. We had already established India, two years prior to this, and in 2012 we had a global client, Nokia, request services from us in other parts of Africa. We had been a long-standing service provider to Nokia in South Africa, and they were managing other territories from a regional office in Johannesburg. The first enquiry came asking us to consider what we could do for them in East Africa. East Africa always appealed to me as a potential market, and a big hub in Africa is Nairobi. It had got plenty of airtime in the last couple of years for its growth, specifically in the IT services space, banking and telecommunications. I had known for many years that Kenya was a very strong contender in the tourism space in Africa with its incredible safaris, coastal resorts and so on.

Kenya however, was also an African market that had been plagued specifically by terrorism. There was the tragic bombing of the US Embassy in Nairobi and several other incidents in Mombasa that really had shaken the tourism industry up there but hadn't had as big an impact in other industrial sectors. When the possibility of looking at an East Africa service contract was first discussed in South Africa, I was very keen because two things had been happening. Firstly, through my church, I had met a couple who had spent many years in Kenya. She was a Kenyan born and bred lady and her partner, or husband, had also done extensive work across the Africa continent, as Africa CEO in a large European engineering firm. So, I had some first-hand contacts at least that I could possibly get some help from, and I might be able to build a network in Kenya off this base. I boldly said to Nokia that I was very keen to get this going and asked what sort of time frame they had in mind. They in turn, wanted to work pretty rapidly on a solution and get moving.

One day, I came out of a Sunday morning service at church and I saw Judy and Hans's son who was looking rather dejected. This young black man had just graduated from a marketing college – he had done a three-year diploma course and had come top of his class. I said to him, "Daniel, tell me, you're not looking good, you're looking a bit down in the dumps, what's going on?" And he explained to me that he was so fired up about his marketing results and so on, but he had been looking for jobs, putting his CV out, going to interviews for the last three or four months, I can't remember how long exactly, but he had kept on being rejected. It was the usual story, they liked him, they liked his CV but he didn't have any experience, also being Kenyan, and holding a Kenyan passport, he didn't really have a work visa and permits that were required to work here in South Africa.

I was just thinking this through when he said, "Uncle Dave, I've even... you know I'd even work for anybody for free, just to get some experience." Having heard that, and his commitment to his own career and journey, it really touched my heart. So I said to him, "Ok Daniel, if that's the case, I'll see you on Monday morning" and he looked at me and asked if I was joking. I replied, "No, I'm not – just come. Come on Monday morning, and work for free, and I will give you that experience." He couldn't believe it – this huge white-toothed smile broke out on his face. He actually didn't know what to say, and I didn't really comprehend what I had just offered him but thought let's get this thing done. Of course I wasn't going to make him work for free, I was prepared to pay him some kind of a stipend starting salary for a young guy like that, but his commitment was not based on any remuneration, his commitment was to get some experience.

In the back of my mind I was thinking: Kenyan, Kenya opportunity on the table maybe... maybe this could be a potential solution. Anyway, he arrived at work as arranged. His mum dropped him off on Monday morning and he started. I introduced him to a few people in my executive and management team and they were startled. They were thinking, "Whoa, what's just happened here, we weren't planning on hiring anybody and now here's this young kid that the CEO has just landed on us. Ag, it's just our crazy maverick CEO up to his tricks again, I don't know how long this is going to last!"

Anyway, Daniel outdid himself and I really didn't do much more than that. I opened a door and he climbed in through that door, boots and all. He charmed everybody in the office; he quickly built up a rapport with everybody, from the tea lady to the South African managing director, and everybody in between. He was bright, he was intelligent, anything that he was asked to do, he did it and more. Daniel impressed everybody with his thoughtful responses to tasks, his questions and so on, and he really made a phenomenal impact. A couple of days later I walked around and I said to a few people, "So, how's Daniel doing, what is he doing? I hope you've given him some meaningful work." All the reviews were great, they were all so impressed. The kind of comments I got were, "Wow, this guy gee, he's taken on so much! He's lightened the load here and he's lightened the load there and he is clever and intelligent. What a great person! What a good guy, where did you get him from? We need more like him..." and so the rave reviews went on.

I'm pleased to say that my sales director Maude also took a shine to Daniel and took him under her wing. She gave him some really interesting things to do from a marketing, sales and general operations point of view. I was so chuffed for him, and he carried on. Two or three months later he had worked his way into the operations team, and he was shadowing an account manager. Daniel was getting stuck in to understanding our technology and how it's used and applied for, or on, our client's behalf. He was getting an understanding of the whole incentive game and the bigger picture, as well as the nuts and bolts and nitty gritty of the incentive process.

It was about the same time, three or four months after he had joined us that the Nokia deal then came to the fore. They were ready to press the button and sign a deal on opening East Africa, Kenya and Uganda. At that stage I asked Daniel how things were going, and would he consider going back to Kenya, and starting Uwin Iwin Kenya? I got that massive Kenyan smile again and I knew he had that challenge already right between his teeth. Now Daniel was all of 23 or something like that, and here he was going to go into Africa back to Nairobi and start a business unit for us. I think everybody was a bit shocked that this was something that I had even considered.

Anyway, a long story short, he couldn't renew his South African visa and he was effectively living in South Africa illegally. So, this was something that he wanted to do anyway or almost had to do. He had to return home to Kenya and now he had this golden opportunity to take, to go and start Uwin Iwin in Kenya. Huw Tuckett, said, "Alright, well I'm going to head up to Kenya with him and establish the business" and that's what we tasked them, Huw and Daniel, to do. Off they went, they found a lawyer and an accounting firm and I made a trip up there as well, and we established Uwin Iwin, Kenya Pty Ltd.

Daniel was operating the beginnings of that business from his home basically, being on Skype, working and getting things established. He was opening bank accounts and registering for local VAT and tax and all of that kind of stuff, obviously with plenty of support from Huw and interaction from myself. With all that put in place, Uwin Iwin Kenya was born. We ran that business unit successfully for three years before Daniel then moved on to another opportunity. It was an incredible story.

Daniel hired a 2IC to do administrative work while he ran around and fulfilled some of the face to face client interaction with Nokia. He was also tasked with trying to look for other business in Kenya, and so he needed an assistant. The Nokia programme grew quite substantially, and a second person was hired so there was a small team of three. Eventually we secured some offices in a beautiful leafy suburb of Kenya, called Karen, Nairobi, we secured this small office in an office park and we got on with things. It was a very successful, profitable little business unit, but unfortunately it was wholly and solely dependent on the revenue of Microsoft and Nokia. After some scouting, we then secured a Kenyan bank, called Chase Bank Kenya, which has nothing to do with Chase Manhattan Bank, and client number two was on board and we were able to get things going. That is the Kenya story in a nutshell, and what follows is Daniel's story.

Daniel – Kenya

This is a brief narrative to the journey to Uwin Iwin East Africa being formed. My journey at Uwin Iwin started off in Johannesburg in April 2012. I had just recently graduated from college and was struggling to find a job mainly because I didn't have any work experience. I happened to share this with Dave who I knew from church, and he was kind enough to give me an opportunity to get some experience at his company. I started off at the marketing department, which was then headed by Leigh Khoza, and she really gave me an insight into the business. We worked together on the Kudosh Card, and pitching that to small businesses, I also got some insight into the events arm of the business, which we also oversaw. After about a month of interning, David and Maud called me in and said they would like me to learn the ropes of sales, and I think it was then really that I started getting much needed experiential learnings from everything that I had learnt in college.

Maud really taught me how to shoot from the hip. She taught me how to sell the company vision from pitch, to a programme getting started, chief of which was the Nokia Ignite programme. I'd really shadowed her when she was putting the proposals together, and as we attended all the meetings with the local office in South Africa, which was fantastic. It was also an opportunity for me to learn the other sides of the business. That had been the sales side, then I was also involved with the merchandise or online team, which was headed at the time by Debbie and Kyle, so I really got to learn so much. Once that programme came into fruition and Uwin Iwin won the bid, an opportunity came for me to go into that online team.

I started working closely with Debbie, who at the time was running the Motorola Incentive programme which was quite successful; it was called Moto Mojo. There was also the Better Bond and there were other automotive programmes running, and of course crafting the Nokia Ignite programme from its inception to it being up and running, so I really got to learn the ropes from Maud and Debbie.

• • • • • • • • • •

After a few months there came an opportunity to grow the East African business. The East Africa Nokia team required an automated incentive programme which was a fantastic opportunity and I remember the day clearly. The South Africa Nokia office was really pleased with the Nokia Ignite programme and there was a conference call that they arranged with the Nairobi team. Essentially, they wanted a replication of the Ignite programme tailored to the Nairobi market. I remember David called me into his car and said, "Come, you are riding with me." We went over to Nando's on Sloane Street and he asked if I thought I could do this and I said, "Yes, why not?" and that was pretty much it, that's what got the ball rolling.

It was a huge blessing. God had set the stage for us, in terms of the exposure I got from Maud, working with the online team, with Debbie, with Kyle and with Catherine. The pieces were all falling into place and I was excited. It was really exciting but very daunting I must admit. I was only a few months, six months at most into my internship. It was a real blessing to go to start off a business with a client in hand, and a fantastic client at that. So based on all the learnings that we got, I moved to Nairobi. That had always been my dream, for a long time anyway and that was on the 12th of October 2012. I was hosted at the field marketing company that Nokia was employing. They had arranged for me to have a desk there so I could easily do training of the sales reps and just start the programme. Three months later, on the 12th of December 2012, which is incidentally Kenya's Independence Day, we launched the programme and that was a baptism of fire if I can call it that.

It was quite a day, all the nerves, all the excitement that comes with it, but it all went well. I remember that by the week before Christmas we had had quite a few sales, we had crossed over the million shilling mark in terms of claims, which was fantastic. That went on and continued to scale through the next few months and in August 2013, there was then the need for the Kenyan programme to be cascaded onto Uganda. By that time I had gotten a second member of the Kenyan office, her name was Caroline Kemani. She was also learning the ropes and so she could manage some of the administrative functions of the Nairobi, or Kenyan programme. I went off to start the programme in Uganda which was all managed remotely from Nairobi, and that also went on to scale nicely.

· · · · ● · ● · ● · ·

In February 2014 we then went into Tanzania which was quite a bit of a challenge because they had completely different dynamics. It was more of an internal or channel incentive programme, but there was of course always the help and support from the SA office in terms of using the learnings that they had, so that went on pretty well. By that time Nokia was pretty much its own machine, it was running well, things were good, and we were now a three-man team. The third person was Grace Minayo, and the ladies were now very good with running the East African programme from an admin perspective. I started looking more towards sales in terms of business development.

As with any cycle, there were now quite a few incentives in Kenya but it was not a very intuitive thing for businesses to take up. It's a very different culture in terms of employment, and there is plenty of skilled labour out there. There are very skilled people and many people with degrees, and big companies don't really feel they have to go the extra mile in terms of rewarding their staff. The consensus is that salary is good enough over reward and that is pretty much the general attitude unfortunately. But to cut a long story short, we had a big win – I managed to get in with

Chase Bank, a fantastic innovative bank that was coming up, charting the way forward in retail banking. They were hungry for anything that would differentiate them from the rest of the banks, and so they took the programme and we started off with a national rewards and recognition programme. The programme was called Chase Chums – Chums being slang for money in Kenya and got an incredible amount of support.

At that time, I was working very closely with Huw Tuckett, and Huw was incredible. He taught me how to think out of the box as cliché as that sounds. He was a pioneer master; I must mention that we also had started off the Nigerian office for the Nokia programme together and we grew quite close. I reported directly to him and he taught me that simplicity is key, but we always need to have a long-term vision of a value proposition that makes sense, and that's the trick of maintaining a business relationship with any client. I'll never forget, one thing he would always, always repeat was how to manage expectations, how to surprise and delight. Working with Huw really helped me craft my managerial skills, how to navigate the ins and outs of boardroom politics, not politics as such but the little nuances that no degree or any kind of tertiary education could prepare you for. These were certain things that he handed over to me that I am grateful for at a strategic level.

· · · ● · ● · · ·

I am digressing, but the point is Chase Bank was quite tough; it was a completely different animal to a sales incentive programme which I thought was what I had. I had really gotten comfortable in terms of understanding, in knowing the cause and effect rules that govern that. Reward and recognition were more long term. There had to be product ownership, there had to be drive from the client, and I think at the time they had so much on their plate and a load of pressure to make this work but there just wasn't that much ownership. Huw and then the rest of the South African team really helped me negotiate those challenges and the uptake of the programme was there during the launch.

It was at that time that we had our 4th person join us, Elizabeth Karanje, a fantastic lady who had worked at Jumia, which is a key digital online ecommerce platform. She now fully owned the Nokia programme. At that time Nokia became Microsoft Mobiles and Elizabeth owned all the incentive programmes and I was focusing on the sales. It was around that time that I started working closely with David after Huw immigrated to the UK with his family. It was beyond incredible to be honest, working with him. David would visit and we would do many of our sales calls together. We visited Toyota which we had worked hard to get, but unfortunately that didn't work out. We pushed quite hard to big printers – Epson, other insurance companies, medical insurance, and so forth and it was amazing for me. David is a master of all trades, everything he does is done with palpable passion; it's done with an attitude of excellence.

• • • • • • • • • •

One thing I love about him is that every time we worked together as a team, it felt like there was no alternative to success, success to the team and success as a whole. We had great synergy, in sales pitches and subsequently developing proposals and just basically answering the needs based on our understanding of what was required. David was amazing, leveraging on our collective local knowledge, things that we could apply from Brazil, India, Nigeria, Uganda and South Africa. He let the clients feel and understand that this expertise would be harnessed into resolving and giving them result-oriented programmes, and that was just incredible. One thing that I must say is that from the get-go, everything that was done was always spirit led. From my time in the Jo'burg office I loved all the prayer meetings that we would have, on a Monday morning as the start of the week. That was something that carried through all the years, the whole time from when I joined Uwin Iwin until the last day – everything was Christ centred, everything was spirit led.

Another thing that I really learned from both Huw and David and of course all the other members was the importance of just living your truth and always having a 'why'. Yes, profit is always the bottom line but we also need to remember that people spend so much more time with their colleagues than they do with their families. The Uwin Iwin vision or goal was to make that time that people spend in earning a living memorable, just by pushing a little. If they push themselves then they can obviously get a bit further in life, whether that be in a monetary or experiential way, and that was incredibly motivating for me.

• • • • • • • • • •

All in all for me, I must say that I need to mention this, David showed me what I wanted, what I wanted to represent without me even knowing or having seen that before, it gave me such a sense of belonging from the first day that I started there. I grew my wings at Uwin Iwin and I really believe that I continued to fly because of the firm foundation that I got from the people that I mentioned, Debbie, Maud, Kyle, Cat, Huw, and of course David. It's been an incredible journey and I know it's not over. Thank you,

I will always be extremely grateful to all of you, and forever grateful for the mantra of always "keep winning".

Forty-Three

Brazil 2016

"Nothing ever goes away until it teaches us what we
need to know." - Pema Chödrön

2016 STARTED OFF WITH the news of the Brazilian economic crisis
looming. There was the impeachment move against the president of Brazil,
Dilma Rousseff, and a messy fight ensued. The crisis in Brazil deepened
and worsened, and it had a similar effect on the currency, which devalued
by almost 30%, corporates and the economy. Corporates were tightening
their belts radically, and we saw some of our key customers in Brazil not
renew their contracts. I knew then that it was going to be a tough year.
Our partners in Brazil kept me abreast of all the goings on but they were
very concerned, not only about their economy but about their own job
security and their own investments. Not only did the corporations tighten
their belts, but banks stopped lending. There was a significant breakdown
in confidence in the business sector and the result was that at the end of
the first quarter, Brazilian corporates really held on to their budgets and
didn't renew contracts.

We had a team of 15 people there, paying salaries and running a nice
office in one of the nicest parts of Sao Paulo, but it just got tighter and
tighter, and we had to cut back. We did several things in the hope of
some kind of recovery in economic stability, but because we didn't have
a significant line of credit and cash flow, we had a reduction from about
seven or eight big corporate blue-chip companies to just two contracts that
remained with us. It was just not sustainable, we had to then immediately
enter a time of downsizing, and retrenching staff which was an incredibly

painful exercise for the local team, and of course for myself from afar. The only real way for the business to sustain itself was for all the partners to chip in a significant amount of equity to cover the costs of the office in its downscaled format for a long six- to seven-month period.

I didn't have the stomach for that and so my CFO, Manus Geyer, and myself, as well as the other board members and the international team did a review. We looked at the risk profile and decided that we wanted to pull out and reduce our risk as minimum. So, we began our exit. We gave the bad news round about July and ceased trading and operation of that entity. It was a huge personal blow to me. We had invested almost three years in trips across to Brazil, plenty of money in start-up capital, as well as some additional seed investment that was lost. We had to boot across about another 50 thousand US dollars to wind up the company as a debt-free asset, as was expected and decreed by the laws of the land.

Anyway, if that was not bad enough, I had other concerns about our African contracts. We were heavily invested into Africa, through the Microsoft supply partnership that we had put in place to service the channel incentives of the Microsoft phone business which they bought from Nokia. That was going from bad to worse and slowly the number and volume of incentive pay-outs and product availability in the markets dropped off. We had established offices in Kenya, Uganda, Cairo, Lagos and Ghana – and month by month the sustainability and return on investment for the business was just no longer there.

Ultimately Microsoft started giving notice, country by country, that our contract would come to an end. First, we dealt with the reduction in contracts for East Africa, Uganda and Kenya, and then we scaled back the Kenyan operation to two staff. One of our founding employees, Daniel Mason, decided to move off to another entrepreneurial opportunity that he had found for himself in partnership with some Danish guys, and we were left with our small office in Karan with Elizabeth and Caroline left to manage the ship. We were hopeful as we had secured a banking contract which had high promise but unfortunately three or four months later that bank went into curatorship. I've never in my life done business with a bank that went into curatorship and become a bad risk client. Anyway, we eventually decided to close the East Africa office and put it into a dormant state because there was no revenue and we had run out of local reserves.

Forty-Four

Egypt

"When you take risks, you learn that there will be times when you succeed, and there will be times when you fail, and both are equally important." — Ellen DeGeneres

OUR OFFICE IN EGYPT was also put on notice by Microsoft. I made one final trip to Cairo, and my dear friend Eslam Mohamed and I resolved to close the business unit there, as business development and economic situations in Egypt were worsening by the day. The new government had not yet delivered on economic growth promises. We had survived the revolution; we had survived the new government getting up on its feet, but we couldn't survive the pulling of our only contract through Microsoft there. We really scrambled around to try to look for another telecommunications business to develop, but we were unsuccessful. Our timing was again not able to sustain the small office that we had developed there, and so we put that business into a suspended trading situation as well in about October 2016.

We also had to put the business in Ghana into suspended trading operation and then had to ask our superstar, Annabelle Kali, to go and find other employment. This was an incredibly sad situation and she had been unable to secure further work.

Thankfully, our South African operation still had great staying power. We had a huge balance of customers in various market segments, and despite the very tough economic trading period of 2016 in South Africa, we managed to do exceptionally well. We grew the business slightly below what we had expected, but nonetheless, it was still a very good and profitable year in 2016.

I must tell you that by the end of 2016 I was demotivated, my morale was down, and I felt rather shaken in terms of my own confidence. But 2016 was particularly difficult for me as I had lost one of my long-standing business partners, Huw Tuckett, late in 2015 as he emigrated with his family to the UK in October. The loss of his support, friendship and incredible managerial operational strength was a major blow to me, and of course, handling all the 2016 issues that I have just described became a monumental burden. Although there were other members in the team that certainly supported me and gave me counsel and guidance, it was certainly a very, very challenging time. By the time I went on vacation on December 15th of 2016, I was absolutely shattered and needed the holiday. I was just so grateful for that holiday and we were able to start in 2017 on a fresh, re-energised different approach. That's where I am going to end the chapter on 2016. It was painful; it was dreadful, but we put in place some of the incredible foundations that I believed would start off 2017 on a solid footing.

Forty-Five

Blessings are New Every Morning

"When you arise in the morning, think of what a precious privilege it is to be alive – to breathe, to think, to enjoy, to love" — Marcus Aurelius

DESPITE THE CHALLENGES WE were having in the international spaces, we were learning so much and growing strong at home. Teams were hitting and exceeding targets and strengthening year after year as individuals grew in confidence and strengths.

Technology was our friend and not foe, so many years of refinement, innovation and happy customers. Our picture was beautiful, our trajectory up and to the right.

Our financial disciplines have never been in better shape and having Manus a fully fledged CA SA at the helm together with a great team, we were starting to refine and master our growth.

Blessings come fresh every day, there is no shortage of opportunity in Africa or anywhere for that matter, it's the brave, the crazy and the energised who chart the entrepreneurial paths and to all of your I say - Keep Winning

Forty-Six

My 50th Birthday Year

"It's not like 50 is the new 30. It's like 50 is the new chapter." – Sharon Stone

2016 WAS MY 50TH year celebration, I was born on the 14th of May 1966. My beautiful wife Dorcas and I planned a real special celebration that took place at our home in Lansdowne Road, Bryanston. The idea was to gather family and friends for an intimate special evening.

This was also the year that I started writing this particular book. I was really motivated to document and tell the story of my life journey to this point in time. For me it was important that my boys have an insight into the blessings the hard work took and the joy that I experienced along that journey.

My wife and her sister-in-law, Stephanie, put in a tremendous amount of work to ensure that the celebration was a happy occasion and met a high standard for such an important life milestone. Planning an event at our home for almost 50 people was not an easy task. My brother Nigel was roped in to help with the catering and my colleague Maud came up with a tremendous entertainer for the evening. It turned out to be such a joyous occasion and every single detail enhanced the experience that I shall never forget. Despite a day that started overcast and raining and continued to rain right through the entire evening we were blessed by friends and family who chose to celebrate this with us. I was showered with amazing gifts and most of all many of our friends and family had such beautiful words to say that touched my heart in a way that lifted my spirits and reminded me of the blessing that they were to me and the blessing I had been to them.

My wife of course spoke of me in a way that honoured our marriage, honoured me and that expressed her gratitude to our two children, Daniel and Nathan, who were gifted to us by God. Daniel and Nathan also stood up and said the most beautiful words, I was so proud of them at that very moment. One of the nicest gifts was a gift that Dorcas and Stephanie designed and created over many days prior was the compilation of a photograph book with the many photographs of people, life experiences, special memories and exotic trips we had taken together. I regularly take a look at that book just as a reminder of how grateful I should be to all the beautiful people in my life, to the career that I've had to date and the incredible spiritual community that I belong to.

This event really spurred me on to take the writing of this book really seriously to share in the most authentic way that I can some of those life lessons learnt along the way, and if nothing else to remind me of the many blessings which I have had in my life and continue to experience.

The process of writing a book is not an easy one and I want to thank Richard Simmons and his partner for helping me along the way. I also want to thank Kim Vermark for helping me get this over the line and publishing the manuscript on Amazon. I have much more to write; I'm now at the age of 57 and so much has happened in these last seven years of my life and the intention is to write a second volume that covers more of my business reflections than my personal life but of course the two are so intertwined it would definitely also have in the book personal stories and reflections no doubt.

I am very fortunate to be in a position now where my almost 30 years' experience in my professional field has gained me the status of a global thought leader in our industry and I am often asked to speak at various local and international events whether they be virtual or in person and this book will also serve to help elevate my personal brand as a speaker, coach, and business leader.

If you have gotten to this stage in the book and have enjoyed it, I really want to thank you for spending some of your lifetime reading and expressing an interest in my life. Life is an exciting, challenging, joyful journey interspersed with some of the most horrendous heart-wrenching and gritty moments. If this book has given you anything I hope that it gives you hope, some new ideas on how to handle challenges, and most of all the courage to keep going, and know that it is not the end until your dreams are realised.

Keep on dreaming, work hard, pursue your dreams, don't do it alone, there's lots of people who can help.

Keep winning.

Lots of love, your friend, David.

Forty-Seven

About The Author

David Sand is a compelling keynote speaker who walks his talk. A respected leader, entrepreneur and authority on performance incentives, David's life and work embody his message. He is a man of heart and action, on stage as much as in person. As founder and chairman of the acclaimed Uwin Iwin Performance Incentives, David has led his team — and clients — to international success. He is a past president of SITE, the Society for Incentive Travel Excellence, a recipient of the IMA Award for Excellence and IMEX Academy Award for his outstanding contribution to the industry. His first book, The Song of the Sandman, thoughtfully documents his journey with valuable lessons from leadership and life.

David also serves as trustee for The Duke of Edinburgh's International Award Foundation's "The President's Award" in South Africa, and chairman of the Scouts South Africa Bryanston First Chapter. Members of his influential international network know David as a trusted advisor, a passionate motivator, and an exceptional golfing companion. But what stands out most is David's values as a leader, a family man and above all, a man of faith.

David's keynotes galvanise audiences with not only inspiration, but also the actionable steps to enhance the way they perform, lead and live.

Audiences Say...... #KeepWinning

"An entrepreneur of note — full of new ideas, always inspired and inspiring... a fantastic speaker and motivator..."

— Arnd Herrmann Managing Director, Eagle Rock Marketing, UAE

"His passion for life and work allow him to inspire...and build trust. "

DavidHornby FIH, Managing Director, Scotland, United Kingdom

"His willingness to listen helps him not only meet my needs but to exceed them. Everything is possible."

Eugene De Villiers ,CEO at Business Events Perth, Australia

"A true leader and visionary."

Dominic Albrecht, Head of Analytics, South Africa

"We need more Davids in this world."

Kerry Botha, CEO, Kerry Botha PR and Communications, South Africa

www.ingramcontent.com/pod-product-compliance
Lightning Source LLC
Chambersburg PA
CBHW071727200326
41519CB00021BC/6606